I Wouldn't Normally Do This Kind of Thing

I Wouldn't Normally Do This Kind of Thing

A Memoir

Marshall Moore

REBEL SATORI PRESS

NEW ORLEANS

Published in the United States of America by
Rebel Satori Press
www.rebelsatoripress.com
Copyright © 2022 by Marshall Moore

This work depicts actual events in the life of the author as truthfully as
recollection permits. While all persons within are actual individuals,
names and identifying characteristics may have been changed to
respect their privacy.

Paperback ISBN: 978-1-60864-161-1
Ebook ISBN: 978-1-60864-162-8
Library of Congress Control Number: 2022945136

To the people of Hong Kong, who have marched in their (our) millions to demand a better system of government and a better future. Many have made extreme sacrifices. Many have gone into exile to protect themselves and their families. Some have lost their lives. Hong Kong was my home for twelve years, and it will continue to be even if I am never able to set foot in the territory safely again. It has been an honor to march alongside you. Gaa yau!

CONTENTS

PART ONE: THE WILD BOY OF AVALON

CHAPTER 1. THE TROUBLE WITH DICK

Pissing sideways isn't my earliest memory. There are a couple of earlier ones, like meeting my maternal grandfather for what might have been the only time. I must have been twelve or fourteen months old. Thirty years older than my grandmother when they got married, Dick (that really was his name) cast a long dour Victorian shadow over my early life via the tendencies toward nutty prudishness and the fear of dentistry he instilled in my mother. In addition to this dim memory of an old man's face, I recall a feeling of deep relevance when I saw him. There might have been light blue walls in the background, but he was backlit, I was a baby, and in all honesty I probably reconstructed these details ex post facto. He died while I was still in diapers, but I have held onto this memory with the same sentiment that keeps me from throwing away the trophy I won in the seventh-grade science fair. He was, after all, the only grandfather my parents allowed me to talk about.

There are other hazy memories, blurs with whispers of meaning. Standing up on the sofa, pulling the curtains open, and looking outside during late fall or early winter. At that time of year in eastern North Carolina, everything turns brown except for the evergreens and the red berries on the holly hedges every other house seems to have. These abject brick ranch houses and bungalows and the grim shrubs around them offer the only color that there is, at least until the orange pumpkins of Halloween have all rotted or been bashed in and the garish strands of Christmas lights go up. The endless fallow fields of tobacco, cotton, soybeans, and corn are drab expanses of grey mud at that time of year. Here and there, you see the nubs of post-harvest corn stalks jutting a few inches up from the ground, or low black tangles of cotton branches with telltale white tufts still clinging for dear life. The flimsy-sturdy tobacco barns sit empty although the honey-dirt smell of the curing leaves has permeated the wood and the flaps of asbestos siding, perfuming the air when you're standing downwind and don't mind inhaling fragrant particles of lung cancer. Meanwhile, the sky looks pounded flat: you're close enough to the grumpy Atlantic that you can feel the dim pull of the water off to the east but you're too far inland to smell the salt and hear the waves crash. The land is flat, greyish brown, and spiked with pine trees. As a toddler I could see all this, and sense it—and perhaps even to some extent understand that these impressions were shaping me—but not articulate it.

So, the pissing. When the time came to graduate from the potty chair to the toilet, my early attempts to stand up like my dad and pee like a man didn't work. The urine seemed to go everywhere but into the toilet bowl. As the owner of the only other penis in the family, the Marine might reasonably have been expected to sympathize. As an ex- fighter pilot who hadn't gotten his head around the "ex" part yet, the Marine saw this as a failure of discipline. When his subordinates fucked up, he barked orders at them. When they later tried to murder him by sabotaging his jet—someone put ball bearings in the fuel tank so that it would blow up upon takeoff—he survived via some combination of luck, spite, and timing. Those dishonorable discharges, he could handle. Mine, not so much. I was not quite old enough to understand what he meant when he barked "Straighten up and fly right!" or "If you don't piss in that commode, it'll be Katy bar the door!" No matter how many times I pointed my ding-dong straight at the toilet, the pee went straight up. Or to the side. Or pretty much anywhere else but where it was supposed to. As for Katy, I had no idea who she was or why she would put bars on the door. The Marine had grown up in a converted chicken coop in the woods outside of Ball, Louisiana: poor white trash from just north of Cajun country, albeit without the exoticizing benefit of one of his extended family's French surnames like Thibodeaux or Delahoussaye. He was an only child because his sister died young and his parents were problematic. What was left of him had PTSD after a couple of unsuccessful attempts to get himself killed flying suicide missions in Vietnam. The Corps sent him back to my mother bodily intact—one of only two members of his squadron who survived, and the only one who came back to the States uninjured, or so the story went—but overlooked or simply didn't care about the howling abyss just under his skin. Laura Mae "Anne Marie" (yes, the quotation marks were on her birth certificate) was not of much help, either. She might have given birth to two children, but I'm not sure she knew how penises worked or had ever seen one close up.

Peeing and flying are not the same thing. Getting a little boy whose dick doesn't work to piss in the john requires patience and nuance and possibly a doctor, not the belt. Toddler me did not want to pee. I would hold it in until my groin ached. Then I'd go: it would cascade down the shower curtain; it would drench

3

the toilet paper; it would puddle all over the floor. Every time a trip to the john went awry, the Marine would glower in disgust and Laura would descend into the hand-wringing Southern Gothic apoplexy that was her baseline under the smiles. Her emotional resting state—a simmering, passive-aggressive rage at having been denied a college education because of her sex (the Dickish ideal of womanhood was a pregnant housewife who could almost balance the checkbook without help from her husband)—simply hadn't prepared her for this. As for me, why I never put two and two together and sat on the toilet to do Number One, I can't say. You have to develop a certain level of abstract thought before this sort of functional flexibility sets in, and I hadn't gotten there yet. So the Marine and Laura fell back on their respective deep-South methods of child-rearing, hoping I'd straighten up and piss right. When the belting and the bleating didn't work, they finally took me to a pediatrician.

I remember him scoffing: *That's easy to fix.* Maybe he didn't say that. Maybe he said something else. The air of scorn was the same. At the time, I assumed his contempt was directed at me, the little boy with the defective ding-a-ling. Why wouldn't he feel that way? After all, I pissed everywhere but where I was supposed to. The attitude lingered, stinging, even if the words themselves are lost in time. As an adult, I've come to wonder if he was annoyed with my parents for letting this go on so long. To clarify, I remember two kinds of language, growing up. There was kid language, which I understood. When my parents spoke to me in the simplified vocabulary and the squeaky, exaggerated tones adults use with little children, I knew what they were saying. When they spoke to each other, or to other adults, I couldn't follow the conversation: they were speaking Grownup Language, which I thought for years was distinct from English. I didn't know all the words, and this caused me no end of anxiety. I detected undertones, hidden meanings, dark currents, but had no clue what I was hearing regardless of how much I tried.

One of these Grownupspeak conversations took place while I lay on the examining table, pantsless. No male human in these circumstances, regardless of his age, likes having his penis discussed so openly, in such concerned tones of voice, in a place where scalpels are present. I didn't *think* they were going to cut it off, but no one told me what was about to happen.

Light flashed off the scalpel. A quick slash was all it took to extend my urethral opening to the spot where it should have been in the first place: right at the tip, instead of a couple of millimeters too low and just slightly too small. The actual name of this condition is hypospadia, and boys born with it piss everywhere but in the commode, although I understand doctors nowadays are more alert to this sort of thing than they were in eastern North Carolina in the early 1970s. Mine wasn't even an extreme case, just a bit of inconvenience. One quick little slice and I could straighten up and pee right after it healed. Isn't modern medicine wonderful? Especially when procedures like this are carried out under anaesthesia, which this one wasn't? I screamed and pissed bloody, scalding urine all over myself, the doctor, the examining table, and presumably everything else in sight. Then I passed out.

Ironically, the solution to one penis-related problem created another: the doctor hadn't given us anything to numb the incision. Laura later told me they were all so traumatized, it probably just slipped his mind. When I tried to relieve myself the next day, that first drop of urine stung like a lit match in the tip of my cock. So I held it until my bladder ached, and when the Marine and Laura saw me with my arms folded over my sore abdomen, they panicked, made some calls, and whisked me off to see another doctor. Appalled at what his colleague had done, this one explained that the other doctor should have given me some medicine for the pain first. He then applied an anaesthetic ointment to the cut.

"After you put this stuff on, wait a few minutes. Then it won't sting when you pee."

The wound healed quickly after that, and there have been no further problems. All the equipment is in good working order. But if we're going to be completely honest, you could say Dick set the tone for things to come.

CHAPTER 2. MY OTHER HEAD

If Dick made my early years a bit troublesome and the later ones worse, the bigger head caused a few problems too. As a toddler, I had a dangerous fondness for swivel chairs. (Doesn't everyone?) Ours were a set of bar stools much taller than I was. I hadn't yet developed the strength and motor skills to climb up into them by myself. That afternoon, Laura picked me up, plopped me onto one, and wandered off to gobble Valium (doctors handed it out like Halloween candy back then) or clean the handgun she kept in her purse or whatever she had to do. Having not yet grown into my propensity to get motion sickness, I loved to sit and spin as fast as the chair would go. Whee! Besides, these swivel stools weren't otherwise comfortable at all: the seats and backs were wooden slats with hard edges and corners. If I couldn't stand to sit still in them long, best to spin around. Back! Forth! Back! Forth! Oops! Something went wrong and I sent myself flying. I still have a mental picture of that split-second, airborne. Shag carpet the color of brick. Low furniture in my peripheral vision, whizzing by. I don't remember landing face-first on the metal slats of an air-conditioning vent. Whatever happened next is gone too. There seemed to be screaming involved, and blood. Laura rushed me to emergency room. She said the doctors were going to sew my head up. But the anaesthetic didn't take: rather than calming me down and dulling the pain, the drug made me hyper, amplifying it. Or so I was later told. More shots. More waiting. More bleeding. Consternation. She made an executive decision and said to get on with it. The docs held me down and stitched me up. I *felt* it and blacked out again.

I probably *should* have had stitches when I fell out of a swing several years later and one corner of the wooden seat bashed my face between my left temple and my left eye. There's still a scar, a little dent in the skin just northwest of my cheek. I got lucky that time: half an inch forward and I'd have lost an eye; half an inch back and I'd have had brain damage or died. We were living in New Bern by then, having moved there from Havelock after the Marine's discharge from the Corps. New Bern's greatest claim to fame is as the home of Pepsi Cola. The town was North Carolina's first proper colonial capital, and served as the state capital for much of the eighteenth century too, but Pepsi's more famous. In fact, one of Laura's favorite fables of personal injustice was her story of typing the manuscript for the first book ever published on the history of Pepsi. The author wrote it by hand, she said, and paid her to turn his stack of chicken-scratch into a legible document. When the book came out, she was appalled to find her name missing from the acknowledgments section. Janelle's and my bloody childhood accidents fell into the same category, personal affronts after *everything she'd done*, injuries that hurt her more than they hurt us. Hadn't she raised us better than that?

Her second-favorite such story concerned childbirth. Mine. As fetuses go, I was a large one. My head, in particular. I have a theory about obstetricians and gynecologists from that era. They were misogynistic sadists who oozed into that line of work because they wanted legal sanction to mangle vaginas.

"You tore me from hole to hole!" Laura would exclaim, beaming at me in a sort of pride I hope I'll never comprehend.

When I was older and she repeated this story for the 19,435th time, I asked why the doctor didn't give her an episiotomy.

"Oh, they said it would heal better if the tear was ragged."

Ours was not a household in which follow-up questions were encouraged.

By the age of four, I had somehow figured out my parents didn't like each other. As with most other moments of emotional clarity in my life, this discovery had no boundaries. It was like watching the sun rise. If you're up at that hour, you set down your cup of coffee, walk across the room, and switch off the light. Regardless of what the almanac says, there's no clear moment of transition; at some point, you just know you've crossed over the threshold of morning. One night I wandered into the den (our houses always had a formal living room full of unpleasant, uncomfortable antique furniture intended for the parties my parents never threw, as well as a den that contained the sofas and chairs that we actually used) and found the Marine and Laura in the middle of a tense conversation. Not an argument exactly, no raised voices, no swear words, just a toxic heaviness in the air like the smell of scorched Crisco in Granny's kitchen every time we visited and she made dinner. I remember a wretched expression on Laura's face and a resigned one on the Marine's.

"Are you getting divorced?" I asked them.

I directed this toward Laura because she didn't belt me when I asked questions she didn't like. Not that her habit of duct-taping my mouth shut and putting me in the closet until she could deal with me again was much better. I could usually more or less breathe but things did get kind of grey and murky

9

after I'd been in there awhile.

"Oh no, of course not! We're just talking," Laura gushed. "We just have to work some things out. But we want to stay together as a family."

The Marine glowered. His other facial expression, blankness, varied depending on the time of day and the number of drinks he'd had. There were gradations. He would stumble home from work in the evening, his face bearing the same thousand-yard stare. After changing out of his work clothes, he would then pour the first of many glasses of scotch on the rocks. The hours between getting home and eating dinner, he'd spend in his blue plaid armchair in front of the TV numbing himself with the booze and the news, bearing witness to the nightly body counts from Vietnam as an act of penitence for having survived. Walter Cronkite and Dan Rather spoke to me more often in childhood than he did.

"When he gets home, don't talk to him," Laura would say. "You don't know what he went through in Vietnam. Never ask him about it."

Later, she asked where my question about divorce had come from. How did I even know what divorce was? Much less guess they might have been discussing it? I couldn't answer then and I still can't.

For all that, the year or so we spent in New Bern might have been the most normal one in my life. I went to preschool at Christ Episcopal Church. Even back then, I had the first inkling I was defective somehow. Something about the way I moved, the way I talked, the way I laughed, as if I were an almost-convincing replica of a human, unnerved other kids. At the same time, everything felt normal because unless you're a refugee or in a war, that's how kids see things. What's around them in that moment is their only frame of reference. Besides, like everybody else at that age, my main concerns at that age were whether Laura would make corned-beef hash for dinner (I hated it) or whether the Marine would lose his shit over some random bit of misbehavior and beat my ass black and blue.

The thing was, I was *special*. That kept being the reason for things.

"You're too pretty to be a boy," Laura liked to say. "When you were a baby, that's what people would always say. They'd see your curly blond hair, come up to me in the supermarket, and say, 'What a beautiful little girl!' When I said you were a boy, they wouldn't believe me. So you know what I did? I pulled your diaper down and showed them your little ding-dong!"

There was even a photo, a Polaroid of me as a toddler standing naked in a plastic kiddie wading pool in the backyard of our New Bern house. I must have been about two. Nothing left to the imagination. She kept that picture handy and was still showing it to people when I was in my teens.

Later, there was the IQ test. I was four when I took it. No one told me I would be taking one. Even if they had, I'm not sure how I knew what an IQ was, much less what the test would entail. Like divorce, it's one of those concepts I acquired through osmosis. It made sense to me that intelligence needed a system of measurement. Everything else did: weight, length, volume, area, temperature. But I thought an IQ test would involve computers and pain. Electrodes inserted through holes in the head. We had computers back in the mid '70s, immense room-sized things that hissed and clattered and beeped. The air in those rooms smelled like a radiantly dusty mixture of rare elements, hot alloys, and the future. Sometimes the Marine brought home the cards the whirring machines ate. You punched holes in them. The holes had to be clean and precise, no little tufts of paper still clinging to the edges of the perforations, or else World War III might start. We also had a lot of Cold War-era spy shows. The Russians had the Bomb and we all knew we could die any minute. I thought an IQ test must be something like brainwashing, during which your captors would saw your head open and pour chemicals in to scrub out your memories and make you do things. The Marine worked with computers and seemed to like hurting me, so of course he'd be a key part of any narrative like that. And that would be the end of me. It would be like the time that doctor sliced my dick open, or that other time one sewed my head shut. Only more so, there would be *brain things,* and I wouldn't get any say in the matter. The Marine and Laura mumbled their vague explanations and took me to a building at East Carolina University. Expecting a science lab, straps, and a bone saw, I was relieved to spend about an hour in a dimly lit room with a man who asked me questions in a low, mild voice. These were similar to the games I played in my workbooks. Complete the picture. What would this object look like if we rotated it. How should these blocks fit together. What do these words mean.

"You aren't going to saw my head open?" I asked.

"Umm… no. I think I need to talk to your mom and dad now, okay?"

I never learned my IQ score. At the time, it didn't occur to me to ask. It seemed I had done pretty well, although something had clearly unsettled my parents. In the same way I intuited they'd eventually get a divorce (I was right), I also subtly realized they were terrified: perhaps not of me, but that they might not be up to the job. A lot had already been thrown at them and here was one more thing they'd have to handle.

Years later, when I asked, they still refused to tell me my score, no matter how persistent I was. It was just a number, they said. It was off-the-charts high, almost untestable, something like the top tenth of one-tenth of one percent, and that was all I needed to know. Their superlatives varied over the years, leading me to wonder how true they were, but the refusal never wavered: I shouldn't dwell on it and they weren't going to tell me. It was just a number I'd be defined by for the rest of my life if I knew it. It would make me arrogant. It would affect all my life choices.

And so it was decided that in the interest of not having the rest of my life defined by a number, I urgently needed to start school right away.

I'd just turned five.

CHAPTER 3. I WAS A FIVE-YEAR-OLD CAFFEINE JUNKIE

We moved from New Bern to Greenville a couple of weeks after I started school at Pace Academy. It had to be a private school because the public ones wouldn't admit a five-year-old. I'm not sure if the move to Greenville happened because the Marine had found a job there, or if he looked for a job there because there was no place in New Bern for me to start school, or both. What I do remember is crawling out of bed at some dark and vulgar hour every morning to eat breakfast and get ready for school. I wasn't a morning person then and I'm still not. When I struggled to get moving at what the Marine called oh-dark-thirty, Laura had the bright idea to fix me a strong café au lait. Hence, I became a caffeine junkie at age five.

I am not sure what I expected my first school to look like, but Pace wasn't it. The schools I'd seen on TV were vast, institutional spaces: endless corridors lined with tall metal lockers, rusty in places, doors warped from years of being slammed shut. The schools I'd seen in New Bern and Greenville might not have been so large (New Bern and Greenville themselves were not so large) but they still gave off the same vibe: prisons without bars on the windows. They looked like they'd smell of armpits and pee. Pace, on the other hand, was out in the country. To get there, we drove out of the city proper, through several miles of tobacco fields, past the fire tower, then up a single-lane paved road into a clearing with pine-forest walls on three sides. The school campus itself was an unimposing cluster of four one-story red-brick buildings that looked like little houses, plus a much larger one I soon learned was the gym. Each building had two classrooms. One grade per classroom; one teacher per grade. We'd spend the entire day in the same class with the same students and the same teacher. This came as a relief. The prospect of changing classes made me nervous. I'd get lost.

School itself was more or less tolerable. With a total class size of about twenty, it wasn't hard to get to know people. Thanks to the miracle of social media, I'm still friends with some of them. A blonde girl named Nancy Cummins and I hit it off right away, and she became my "girlfriend" almost from the start. A blond boy named Julian Perkins seemed to hate me from day one. But I made friends with a few others—Scott Newton, Bruce Koonce—to keep life sort of bearable. I got up early in the morning, drank my coffee, got in the car with the Marine, and did it all over again. Now and then bigger thoughts crossed my mind: Was this what adulthood would be like? The morning routine, the travel, the fatigue at the end of the day? These thoughts would not stay in my head long; I was five and everything was new.

Routine ruled each day. Our morning English lessons had a heavy focus on grammar (I might even still know how to diagram sentences) plus vocabulary and spelling. We'd have recess around 10.30, for about twenty minutes. Before lunchtime, either math or geography. Lunch at our desks. Everyone had their own lunchbox. In each lunchbox, there would be some variation on the same sandwich. No refrigeration, but this was the mid-'70s, after all: the luncheon meat contained so many preservatives that if we hadn't eaten it, it would still be a stack of unspoiled pink protein circles in a plastic package today. Afternoons weren't so bad: lessons for another hour and a half or so, social studies and maybe science, and then the bell would ring at 2.30, setting us free.

We didn't stay in our first Greenville house very long, maybe a year. The Marine and Laura bought one in a new neighborhood just outside of town in a development called Avalon. I remember picking out the color for the carpet in my bedroom. I chose chocolate brown because it seemed very adult.

"Don't you want something... sporty?" Laura asked hopefully.

Even at that age, I was already wondering when she would notice that there was nothing sporty about me. My utter lack of coordination meant I couldn't throw or catch a ball to save my life.

"Can I have black?"

"Oh God no. It'll show dirt."

"But brown's okay?"

Brown was okay.

Afternoons in Avalon would have been idyllic if we'd been around to enjoy them, but since both parents worked, Janelle and I went straight from school to a daycare center for the rest of the afternoon. If Pace Academy (which the other kids seemed not to have heard of) was a known quantity, predictable and therefore sort of comfortable, the daycare centers (we went through a succession of them) were about one step removed from state orphanages. Run with the sort of impersonal care that pet-shop staff offer puppies and kittens awaiting adoption, these places sped up the onset of my major depression by quite a few years.

Since the women who worked there would come looking for anyone who tried to hide, I hit upon the idea to make our own imaginary houses right out in plain sight. Janelle and I would retreat to one corner of the sandy backlot, and I'd make a raised barrier of sand, a right angle connecting the two sides of the fence, by taking half-steps and pulling my feet together. Since there always seemed to be floorplans of houses lying around, I understood the idea of diagrams for living spaces. Creating my own to put some psychological space between us and the rest of the watery moles only made sense. If we couldn't physically leave, we'd tune everyone else out. We'd sit in our "house" and play by ourselves, or just read.

"Don't you want to play with the other kids?" the daycare workers would occasionally ask.

We'd look around at them, doubtful.

"No, thank you."

I'd read. Janelle had her dolls, or her homework. It was enough.

Now and then, some of the kids would climb over the fence because of the Fast Fare convenience store next door. I think they did it just to get away from the boredom and the sour smell of baby piss. They'd go in to buy soft drinks and candy. The manager would call the daycare center. The kids would be rounded up, brought back, yelled at, and made to sit in corners.

Since it was essential that my life not be defined by a number, the Marine and Laura decided I needed even more math! More vocabulary! More everything! (In fairness, I did enjoy reading the dictionary.) The downside of being intellectually gifted and having insecure, mentally ill parents of modest means is that they tend to go overboard in their efforts to force you to have a better life than they did. At some point while I was in the first grade, the Marine bought a couple of more advanced elementary-school math workbooks, and began forcing me to study after dinner.

"You need a challenge!" he liked to say.

There are only so many times a five- or six-year-old kid with a long commute can do addition and subtraction before getting bored and starting to fidget. And I couldn't figure out less-than and greater-than, no matter how many times he and Mrs. Williamson (my first-grade teacher) and later Mrs. Gallagher (my second-grade teacher) tried to explain them. What did < and > mean? Mrs. Williamson tried to explain it by comparing the symbols to alligator mouths. Not helpful. When I couldn't be made to get it (in college, I would learn that because of my age, my brain was not developmentally ready to understand those concepts), the Marine took to slamming my face into the pages of the book.

"You're not trying! You need a challenge! You're not being challenged!"

Irony was never his strong point.

When I finished one supplemental math book, the Marine bought more at Rose's, a long-gone local predecessor to Walmart and Target. I would tag along, resigned, dreading the extra time I'd have to spend working math problems at the kitchen table under ugly yellow light. The challenge wasn't the times tables or the division, it was just figuring out how to manage the Marine as he sat there drinking scotch and glaring at me. If I said the wrong thing, he'd clap his hand around the back of my head and whack me facedown against the table, never quite hard enough to break my nose or leave a bruise, but enough to leave a stinging red patch that would fade to an ache in half an hour or so.

He rarely talked about his own life as a kid, but now and then he'd drop a little truth bomb: "I grew up in a converted chicken coop in the woods outside of Ball, Louisiana," he'd say, always the same preface to the few stories he'd let himself tell. He still had his central Louisiana accent, which at the time I didn't recognize as heavily seasoned with Cajun. I'd never been there, never met any of the relatives I assumed I must have. "Do you understand that? We didn't have a house. We lived in a camper, and later in a chicken coop. I didn't have the opportunities you have now. You better straighten up and fly right, or it'll be Katy bar the door."

Janelle had to do these things too. Supposedly her IQ was as high as mine, but she had the potential to be even more successful in life: she had my mistakes to observe and to learn from. Therefore, she was forced to study too, but the Marine and Laura didn't push her as hard. On the one hand, it's true that second children are sometimes more socially successful than their firstborn siblings. On the other hand, I've often thought that her lazy eye and her cataract set her up for the crisis of low expectations people with disabilities tend to face; as if the fact that one eye didn't work meant her brain also didn't.

There were always other things hanging in the background. We were constantly talking around them but we weren't allowed to ask direct questions. Sometimes I wondered why the Marine came home, poured his first drink, and kept refilling his glass until at least nine or ten most nights. Why he hit us, why it involved the "go pick out a belt" ritual. Why there were so many guns in the house. Why other people knew their grandparents and we didn't.

The Vietnam War finally wound down. Of course, I knew

very little about why we had been there in the first place: something about communism, which we'd been taught was an evil system of government bent upon unleashing totalitarian hell on earth. The Marine had been in Vietnam *twice* for some reason, and we weren't supposed ask why, even if we understood that military guys didn't normally sign up for second tours of duty. In hushed tones, Laura would repeatedly caution Janelle and me against asking him questions. It was so terrible, she'd say in low tones, he can't talk about it. He's not okay. He needs time. He loves you very much, and it's important to discipline your children. We managed to get a few stories of stories out of her (he'd taken a shit-dipped *punji* stick through his foot, pulled it out clean, and survived; everyone else in his squadron been killed or critically injured, and he had survivor's guilt; somebody had sabotaged his jet in a murder attempt), but we were under no circumstances to press him for details.

This was when I began to worry about the draft. I knew at the age of five or six that I was still years from having to worry about being drafted. Even so, the idea that the government could ship young men off to Vietnam for murky reasons to die awful deaths in the jungles was appalling. It clashed with my idea of what America was supposed to be about, too. Land of the free, home of the brave? How exactly did freedom entail being sent off to some jungle in another country to get a turdstick through your foot? That didn't sound brave to me, it sounded stupid. Wasteful. Throughout elementary school, this was where my head was. I'd seen the body counts on the news every night; I brooded over it.

Defending your country: I kind of got that. Like if the Russians invaded. But how did fighting in Vietnam make America safer? We didn't seem to have won the war, either, although nobody wanted to say so back then. And if the Marine's temper was any indication, fighting over there had messed people up psychologically. He was always grim, always drinking at night. We had to be quiet and do our homework (or our extra homework). If we pissed him off, he'd snap. He'd get the belt or whatever else was handy. There were always a couple of yardsticks around, a wooden one and a metal one, and I think he once used an electrical cable. The rational part of him switched off, and if we screamed enough while he was hitting us, eventually it would resume functioning.

My doubts about Vietnam gave way to other doubts. Brainwashing was a common theme of TV shows and movies back then. Evil spies were always kidnapping heroes and heroines and brainwashing them via techniques similar to IQ tests, but in reverse. *The Six Million Dollar Man* and *The Bionic Woman*, for example, illustrated just how much danger still lurked in the world. Drills and electrodes; scary drugs and mind control. I didn't want to be brainwashed, and reciting the Pledge of Allegiance every day at school began to feel like brainwashing. I didn't even understand it for the first couple of years of school:

- *I plejja leejance tootha FLAG* (Oh, wait a minute, that's *to the flag*)
- *AntootharePUBLICforwichitSTANDS* (Public? Re? *Public* isn't a verb so how can you do it a second time? And *stands*? What stands?)
- *ONE NATION UNDER GOD* (I understood that part, but not the usage of *under*)
  - *Indivisible* (Was that like *invisible*?)
  - *Withlibertyanjustissferall.* (Huh?)

As I got older and began to understand the more abstract

concepts like pledging allegiance and liberty (I had previously only thought of Pledge in terms of the lemon-scented wood-cleaning spray Laura used on the furniture), I began to feel quietly outraged. It was Brainwashing Lite, no question about it. Having to repeat the words every day must mean we were being trained to believe them, and I wanted to be left alone to come to my own conclusions. I couldn't have explained my feelings then, had anyone asked, and an atavistic hunch cautioned me not to talk about them. So I started mouthing the words to the Pledge. No one knew. At night, I did my math problems. At school, I got As and scored in the 99th percentile and generally aced everything that was thrown at me, even though I believed in none of it. Even at that age, faking it was easier than picking out a belt.

CHAPTER 4: CINNAMON EYE

At the intersection of E. 10th Street and River Bluff Road, three parking lots emptied into the same blind spot, and there was only a stop sign to regulate the traffic, not a light. A few years earlier, a professor at East Carolina had been flattened there while riding his bike to work. This rainy morning in early July, I had just turned six. Janelle and I were bickering as usual while Laura drove us to daycare before going to work. The rain had given way to a drizzle, but the road was still slick. Laura stopped as the car ahead turned left into the lot shared by a convenience store and a branch of the state Alcoholic Beverage Control store (in North Carolina, you can't buy liquor at the supermarket). The car behind us was speeding, though, and so was the car behind *it*. I had climbed into the back of the wagon to get away from Janelle, who stayed in the back seat. Laura had one of those vast, yacht-like Ford station wagons, meaning I could put some distance between myself and my nuisance of a little sister.

The first time we were rear-ended, I didn't know what had just happened. There was a loud jolt. It was over before I even realized we'd been hit. The car bounced off our back bumper, no major damage done. It would have taken a pretty hard impact to have dented that big old Ford station wagon, one of those '70s-era gas-guzzlers the size of a houseboat. And that is precisely what happened next. The car behind the first one that hit us was speeding too, and the driver didn't stop in time. I think he hit the brakes at the very last second. The impact slammed the car behind us into us again. This time, the rear window exploded, peppering my face with safety-glass buckshot. I sat on a larger shard and cut my ass too, but didn't know that until later.

The back seat folded down on Janelle, protecting her from damage. I think she ended up with one bruise.

When I climbed out of the car, I had my left hand clamped over my left cheek. A concerned-looking woman with shoulder-length blonde hair asked me if I was okay.

I nodded and asked her, "It's raining. Why are you holding your shoes?"

She pointed at her mangled Volkswagen Beetle. She'd made the mistake of turning right just at the time of the second impact.

"The wreck tore them off my feet," she said. "They're ruined."

"You're lucky you still have feet."

Laura, standing next to her in the rain, was ashen.

"Take your hand away from your face," she said when she could talk again.

I didn't want to. I didn't know why, but it seemed very important for my hand to stay where it was. Blood had begun to drip from beneath it. I was dimly aware of this, even if I couldn't feel it.

"Take your hand away from your face!" Laura screamed.

When I did, a little jet of blood spurted out of my cheek. And then another. And then another. Laura later said this occurred in time with my heartbeat.

"I can't feel anything," I said.

"It's because you're shocky," she explained. I had no idea what that meant, and she repeated it several more times anyway as we waited for the ambulance: "You're shocky. You're shocky. You're shocky."

Within minutes, an ambulance arrived. Being Southern, everyone involved pronounced it *ambu*-lance (think *dance*, not *dunce*). Blood continued to leak down my chin until the paramedics put some gauze over it. I hoped I wasn't cut badly enough to need stitches but I had a bad feeling about the wound on my face. No one would give me a mirror.

At the hospital, the doctors took one look at me and said *papoose board*. I asked what that was. When they told me, I screamed, "Don't put me in that!" This is the moment that made me hate being a kid. I understood why I was in the emergency room. I understood that they needed to fix my face, give me stitches, whatever. I understood the concept of anaesthetics and the necessity of lying still. As the doctors and nurses lowered me onto the board and laced up the straps (Velcro had either not been invented yet or wasn't in widespread use), I didn't budge. I had a point to prove. Offended and infuriated, I swore like a baby stevedore throughout the procedure (as usual, the painkillers only kind of worked): *"Shit! Damn it, you asshole! Shit, what are you doing?"* Not bad for a six-year-old still some years away from mastering English's finer vulgarities. I'd have called the surgeon picking bits of glass out of my face much worse if I'd known stronger words yet. The doctors chuckled while I cussed them out; afterward, they said I'd been a better sport than most kids my age. Most kids wiggled and fought, they told me. I hadn't. I only glared at them, still livid but also grimly satisfied, knowing I had made a point.

A persistent dull pain in my butt began to bother me. My face was such a mess that no one had noticed the bloodstain on my ass: I'd sat on some glass.

"My butt hurts," I said to the Marine, who had finally arrived.

He took me to the nearest men's room. I pulled down my pants and he took a look. Back to the operating table I went, but at least the doctors didn't strap me down this time. Fortunately, the cut—superficial—only needed a few swabs of Betadine and a bandage. No stitches. Still, the humiliation of being on yet another operating table with my pants down and a bunch of bemused adults standing around burned like the medicine they cleaned the wound with, and I didn't talk for a while after that.

When during all of this did Laura start talking about plastic surgery to repair the scar on my left cheek? (Face, not ass.) Maybe before we left the emergency room; maybe when we went to the doctor a couple of weeks later to have the stitches pulled out.

"Plastic surgery?"

Plastic wasn't alive. Why would it need surgery? *Surgery*, I understood. That was an operation. I couldn't decide whether I'd just had one. Did having bits of glass plucked out of your face count as an operation, or was it just sort of a repair job? Having an operation sounded both glamorous and unpleasant: glamorous in the abstract, but unpleasant in that it might involve blood, pain, and papoose boards. But *plastic* surgery? Laura tried to explain. I was going to have a scar on my face after this, maybe a big one. When I grew up, there would be insurance money for me to have it removed.

"They can do that?"

"Yes."

"How?"

"Well, it's like your father's tools. They can sand it off your face with a special machine. It uses very fine sandpaper. Or they can peel off the skin…"

I was several years away from knowing how to say *fuck that* (despite my love of swearing, I don't think I learned the word "fuck" until I was in the fifth grade), but already old enough for the sentiment to be there.

"I'm keeping the scar."

"*What?* Why?"

"It would hurt."

"But they'd spray something on it so you wouldn't feel anything. Or they'd give you a shot…"

Not better.

"I'm keeping the scar."

I wouldn't budge on that point. After the swelling (kids at the daycare center called it the "goose egg" and me "cinnamon eye" because my eyeball had filled up with blood; later I found out I was lucky not to have gone blind in that one), the wound with its lattice of stitches looked kind of like a small black-and-red Chinese dragon on my left cheek. It made me look tougher than I felt on any given day. I was already aware of being something of a disappointment—they had both wanted a jock and had gotten a clumsy, prissy nerd—and the injury gave me a tough edge I otherwise lacked.

"You may feel differently when you get older," Laura said in the smug *I'm your mother and I know more than you do* voice I hated.

"I won't," I said.

I still have the scar, a faint, jagged little line across my left cheek. You can see it when the light hits it a certain way. There's still a tiny speck of glass under the skin, too. The surgeons missed it. Even now, more than forty years later, if I press a finger against it, it stings.

CHAPTER 5: TWO FUNNY UNCLES

Eventually the Marine and Laura relented and let us quit daycare, figuring we were old enough to look out for ourselves at home. In the living room in the back of the house, we'd sit on the overstuffed goldenrod-colored sofa watching our drip-feed of normal on TV. Janelle would bump. She claims I'm the one who thought it up, and she picked up the habit from me, although I'm not clear on how old we were at the time. Five and three, maybe? Six and four? She'd lean forward in whatever chair she was in (an armchair, the sofa, a car seat, even movie seats if she got bored with the film), pivot at the hips, bounce off the back of the chair, and do it again: bump bump bump bump. How she could follow the stories on TV with that habit, I never knew. In retrospect, I think the whole point was *not* following TV shows—or anything else in her surroundings. Eventually she'd tire herself out and fall asleep. As a little girl with a vision-related disability, always being told "no, you can't do that but Marshall can," Janelle saw through the fake normalcy years before I did. Outside of school, she was always either bumping or sleeping, at least until she got older and discovered drugs.

As time went by, afternoon cartoons like *Tom and Jerry* gave way to syndicated reruns (*Bewitched, Dark Shadows, Gilligan's Island, Star Trek*). Of the three, channel 12 (ABC) had the best shows, but we lived too far from the station in New Bern to get good reception. Half the time, it was static and snow. Sometimes we could get PBS—channel 5 out of Raleigh—but most of what we saw on that station involved adults with big hair talking to each other. Even the static on the empty channels was more entertaining. When we weren't in the mood for TV, we'd go outdoors and play, and some days I would range deep into the woods surrounding our neighborhood, only stopping when the ground became too swampy for me to continue on. I once tried using the cypress knees that jutted up from the dark, brackish water as stepping stones, but they hurt the soles of my feet.

Outwardly, everything looked an updated version of Norman Rockwell's America: white middle-class mother and father, nice house in a respectable subdivision just outside of town, two (extremely) academically gifted kids. There were drives through eastern North Carolina's endless countryside (now and then we had to roll up our windows because of the stink of livestock shit from the farms or wood pulp from the big Weyerhaeuser mill on the way to New Bern) and trips to the beach (I once put a sand flea down the back of Janelle's swimsuit, it got into her vagina, and Laura had to help her pull it out). Cute gift shops in historic towns like Bath and Belhaven. Seafood dinners in waterfront restaurants. Weekend visits to New Bern to see Granny.

This was also our normal, middle-class white America: Janelle, bumping and sleeping all the time, so much so that at least one doctor warned the Marine and Laura about these habits. The Marine, stumbling in sometime after five, changing clothes, and sinking into his armchair with drinks and TV. Laura, heating up canned vegetables and baking pork chops after stumbling in after her own job. She drank at least as much as he did but hid it better. Someone was finishing those jugs of Taylor Lake Country White and it wasn't Janelle and me. Our normality was the day she broke down sobbing in the kitchen: "Sometimes, I just want to get in my car and drive away and never see any of you again!" Or me noticing one day that it had been a few years since she'd last taped our mouths shut and put us in the closet so she could read. I didn't ask her about it because I didn't want to put ideas in her head. I figured I'd grown too big for that to happen again, but she might think of something else. Besides, hadn't everybody's dad had come back from Vietnam messed up? Wasn't everybody's little sister a tiresome, tag-along little rage blob? Didn't everybody have to move the gun and the bottle of pills aside when they went looking for the cuticle scissors or the box of Tic-Tacs in their mother's purse? The Marine and Laura didn't socialize, and we didn't go spend the night at our friends' houses very often. We had no idea how other people lived, only what we saw on TV.

We weren't allowed to shut our bedroom doors at night. We knew the Marine was hard of hearing, but we didn't talk about that either. He told us that when he was a teenager, someone had shot a gun too close to his head. Officially this was not a murder attempt, but in our family you never knew. Then, later, he was too close to explosions in Vietnam. If anything were to happen, if there were some sudden emergency, he wanted to hear us. Which made no sense whatsoever: he couldn't hear when he was awake, so what good was this supposed to do in the middle of the night? Besides, Laura had always assured us she was telepathic, carefully monitoring everything we thought and did. She would make sure we didn't do anything bad and nothing bad would happen to us because her clairvoyance enabled her to see what we were up to at all times.

"Sometimes your father's thinking about what to have for dinner, and I'll buy it the store on the way home and cook it for him," she would say.

"You always know what we're thinking and what we're doing?"

"Of course."

For me, though, normal felt like something to aspire to. I didn't outgrow the sense that my body didn't work the way boys' bodies were supposed to. I moved like an ill-fitting assemblage of spare parts. When I walked, the Marine would sometimes snarl "Stop sashaying around like a girl!" or "Stop switching your ass!" One time, having misunderstood, I looked up "sachet" in the dictionary. According to Merriam-Webster, a sachet was a small packet of something: spice, perfume, powder. I didn't understand how walking like a girl involved sachets, unless they would begin to fall out of my ass if it swung side-to-side enough. If in an absent moment my wrist went limp and my hand dropped, the Marine would explode. Once when he and Laura were looking at buying a garden shop, my handshake with the owner was too faggoty for his liking: I sort of grasped the man's fingers and curtsied. I'd never been taught how male handshakes worked. Later, amid all the screaming, I wondered how I was supposed to get gestures and movements like these right when I was only ever yelled at and beaten up for getting them wrong without ever having been shown what to do in the first place.

"He's so tall!" the people we met would sometimes remark. "He should play basketball."

Balls I threw didn't go very far, and when the time came to catch them, I tended to duck or scoot out of the way. Soccer lessons didn't work out much better: I wore sandals to practice one time and tore a toenail half off. The coach looked at me with the same disgust I saw at home on the Marine's face, and I quit the next day.

Alone in my room, I would practice walking. Back and forth across the chocolate-colored carpet, concentrating on my hips. I don't know if I succeeded in stabilizing my butt, but the screaming eventually stopped. It's more likely that I trained myself to walk like a stork or a flamingo, one of those birds with long skinny legs, a bulbous body, and a beak.

My accent seemed to annoy people too. Being hard of hearing and from central Louisiana, the Marine had peculiar ways of saying things. Lacking the sharp tones of the Upper South, his speech was more of a slow drawl, drawing out different syllables. "Guarantee" came out as "guar-AWN-tee," for example. "Louisiana" was "Looziana." He mangled "faggot" too. It came out sounding like "faggist" when he said it. "Faggist": one who fags, or is disposed to faggotry, which he clearly thought I was.

"Oh, don't worry about that," Laura tried to console me one time when I brought up the word people at school were calling me. "We know you're not like *that*. We've already discussed it. When you're old enough, your father's going to take you to a whorehouse to make a man out of you."

The other part of my accent that people couldn't abide was the High Tider half. Granny had grown up in Hyde County, population less than 10,000. There might be one stoplight in Swan Quarter, the county seat. The rest of it's marshland and subsidence. The whole county's below sea level and floods when hurricanes come through. The English spoken there and on the Outer Banks is known as the High Tider dialect. More than an accent, it's a sublimely chewy flavor of English that

33

churns the words "high tide" into "hoi toide." "Hyde County" becomes "Hoide Cunty," because of course it does. The extreme isolation of North Carolina's mainland coast and barrier islands prevented much interaction with the rest of the world, resulting in this linguistic fly in amber. Although Granny had lived further inland, in New Bern, for most of her life, some of those vowel sounds lingered in her speech and found their way into mine. At some point my not-walking-funny project turned into my not-talking-funny project: I got a tape recorder and started recording myself, practicing behind closed doors, trying to flatten out my drawl and sound like a normal person.

We had no idea how the Marine's family talked because we'd never met them. There were no family stories to speak of, not on his side. We knew he had a younger sister who died of spinal meningitis at the age of five. In fact, that was part of what drew my parents together. Laura had a baby brother who died in the crib. But that didn't come up until later. Both engaged to other people when they met, they hit it off at an officers' ball at Cherry Point: he a fighter pilot, dashing in his officer's whites; she a darkly pretty secretary still living at home with her parents. She stepped on his toe while they were dancing, and made a pert remark. Drunk, he turned her over his knee and administered a good spanking—in front of everyone.

Laura burst into tears and wailed, of all things, "I'm going to marry you for that!", then made good on her threat.

Exactly how she broke off her engagement to Joe and how the Marine cut loose his fiancée in Louisiana has never been clear to me. But they did, on a whim, only a couple of months after they met. Laura always loved this story for its element of mad, naughty romance; by the time I got old enough to enjoy Robert Heinlein, I came to view it as the nexus on the present dark timeline. Beyond that elementary framework, though, it was one of many topics I learned not to ask about. I knew that Joe had curly hair like mine, so from an early age I suspected (and later hoped) he might be my biological father. Since the Marine never got around to having the birds-and-bees talk with me, I was murky on the precise nature of those transactions. One night I asked about that at dinner. I asked, "I thought I got my curly hair from Joe?", the Marine slammed his hand down on the table, got up, and stormed out of the kitchen. One more topic joined the list of Things We Must Never Bring Up.

Since it was crucial for me to be normal and I clearly wasn't, Laura told me a few stories. Turns out I had two funny uncles, one on each side of my family: the Marine's uncle Rudy and Laura's cousin Bonnie (yes, Bonnie was a man). They lived with a surprising degree of openness, given the Southern locale and the times (the forties, fifties, and sixties), but scandal surrounded them like a malaria-cloud of mosquitoes.

I met Uncle Rudy (who was also my godfather) briefly, when I was a toddler. He lived in Northern Virginia by then. I have dim memories of a grand house, a dinner with food I didn't recognize and probably didn't eat, and a toy message board with felt letters to play with when I got bored. When I try to remember what Rudy looked like, nothing concrete comes to mind. I was too young to comprehend and retain much of what I saw; later, I may have seen pictures of him, but when you're young, everyone in black-and-white photos looks old, and the same. Besides, the felt letter-board toy was more fun than the adults in the room. Bonnie I never met; he died a decade or two before I was born, but I heard about him often enough.

Rudy was a friend to both of my parents, the Marine in particular. A member of that generation of gay men and women who migrated to major cities after serving in World War II, Rudy met the man who would come his partner (I don't know his name) during the war; they settled in Fairfax, not far from the District of Columbia. They owned an antique shop. And he took the Marine under his wing from an early age. In a post-divorce email, the Marine told me Rudy had often sent him books, the intention being to open his eyes to the world outside of Ball, Louisiana. Throughout the sixties, the Marine stayed in touch with Rudy and made an effort to visit, long after the rest of the Moore clan had washed their hands of him in good Christian disgust. He even took the Marine to a couple of DC gay bars. One visit resulted in a man who had been flirting with my father getting a black eye for his efforts. Rudy, the Marine could deal with. Other fags, myself included, not so much.

On Rudy's deathbed (his partner had predeceased him), or so Laura told me with appalled giggles, he asked my parents to clean out his personal effects before his relatives from Louisiana raided the house and saw anything they shouldn't. Laura told me this story several times when I was a kid, her eyes wide in titillated horror as she described handcuffs, dildos, and pornography depicting acts she'd *never even heard of!* Rudy wanted to leave my parents everything (his antiques, not the smut), but no will could be found. The Louisiana Jesus contingent who had long ago turned their collective back on him descended on his house like a biblical plague of locusts and made off with the White House china, the silver, and countless other heirlooms. Rudy's sisters had already conveniently whisked him from Fairfax back to Louisiana to "take care of him" in his final illness, so there wasn't even time to say goodbye before he died. I hope they poisoned him with something fast-acting instead of forcing him to marinate in righteous Southern hatred in his final weeks, but there's no way of knowing what the end of his life was like.

At the time, the Marine (still an active-duty pilot) was stationed in North Carolina. In an email, he told me that when he died, the family in Louisiana could not wait to get Rudy buried. They intended to do it the next day. The Marine only made it to the funeral because his commanding officer let him borrow a plane. He made it to Louisiana in two hours and took a taxi straight to the funeral home.

Laura had fewer stories to tell about Bonnie. According to family legend, her forebears had once owned most of the land around what is now Havelock, via grants from the Crown. The deeds themselves remained in the family but most of the property didn't. Bonnie tore the royal seals off the land grants and sold them, Laura said, not only ruining any claim the family might have had to property, money, or public recognition, but also destroying the documents, which would have been heirlooms of some value in their own right. As if all this weren't enough, she made him sound like a flaming deviant with the intellectual capacity of a bag of dead butterflies. Shuddering, she told me how he'd arrange for her to catch him *playing with himself* when she spent summers with her aunts. She'd walk into the room and there he'd be, shorts pulled down and touching his *thing* and leering at her. He got in trouble with the law multiple times for petty theft, lived with his mother all his life, and died a pathetic male spinster.

She was never specific on details of any romantic interests he might have had, because that wouldn't have served her purposes. She made a horrible tautology out of his story: Rudy was gay. Bonnie was gay. Rudy did creepy, disgusting sex things. Bonnie was bad, and an idiot. Gay was bad. Don't be gay, because if you are, this is the kind of life you're going to have. Be normal, like we are.

CHAPTER 6: SPLONDORIOUS

We hadn't been living on Fox Haven Drive very long, maybe a couple of years, when one Saturday afternoon in late winter we went for a long drive down into the swampy murk of Hyde (or possibly Carteret) County. It had rained, and a low layer of clouds lingered like a cold that won't go away. Grey skies, black trees, and the kind of clammy chill that soaks in and hints that the thermometer is lying. Mud squelched under the little Datsun's tires, and I worried/hoped we'd get stuck out in the middle of nowhere. It would be an adventure. We'd been in the car at least an hour, mostly not talking. Janelle and I passed some of the time with a game of Beetle-bug, a contest to see who could spot Volkswagen Beetles. When you saw one, you had to say "Beetle-bug white!" or "Beetle-bug green!", and there were bonus points for spotting a convertible ("Converta-bug yellow!"). Time passed; we crunched up that back road and came to a stop on a rise overlooking an expanse of mud and nothingness. The Marine and Laura had inherited it, although I could never work out who the deceased party was or how we were related. There seemed to be a loose constellation of distant kin scattered up and down the Outer Banks and the inland coast, in towns like Duck and Engelhard and Pantego, but apart from Granny's two surviving brothers and their families, Janelle and

I never met them. In short order, the Marine and Laura sold the land and put the money toward building a new house, hiring an architect friend in Raleigh to design a modern 5000-square-foot saltbox.

Things began to happen rather fast. The Marine and Laura purchased a sloping lot—with a pond! And ducks!—in Brook Valley, one of Greenville's two country-club neighborhoods. (Laura nicknamed it "Broke Valley" and tried for years to milk the joke for a laugh.) The site was staked out; excavation began in a clearing in the center of the property. Behind the big square where the house would go, there was a stand of trees not extensive enough to be called a forest but too dense to walk through without getting cut to shreds in the curtains of briars. Behind that, our land ended and the golf course began. There was another pond back there—a water trap—and two manicured fairways. As for the house, it was going to be what Laura called splondorious: the ground floor would be an immense drive-in basement with enough space for the Marine to have a woodshop and Laura to have a gardening stand. On the first floor, there would be three rooms almost large enough to qualify for their own area codes: a vast kitchen with a walk-in pantry, a similarly enormous den, and a formal living room for the stuffy Duncan Phyfe antiques we seemed obliged to own but rarely used. There would also be a half bath, a couple of storage closets, and a small office for Laura. Upstairs, an archipelago of bedrooms—including one for Granny, with its own en suite bathroom—and the laundry room. And the third floor contained a playroom for Janelle and me as well as the entrance to the attic. Splondorious!

We weren't rich, but as the house took shape and grew skyward, there were moments when it felt as if we were.

Noticeably larger than the others on the street even before it topped out but mostly hidden behind the stand of trees at the front of the lot, the house attracted attention: drivers passing by would slow down to gawk. This didn't last long, though. Before the contractors finished building, something went wrong between the Marine and his architect friend. Suddenly he wasn't on the job. It seemed they'd hired him without a formal contract. There was something about money. Had we run out of it? Had the architect spent it all? I couldn't tell, and when I walked in on their hushed, bitter discussions, the Marine and Laura wouldn't say. On weekends and after work, the Marine began working on the house by himself. The workmen still came during the week, and the Marine continued the work on weekends. Sometimes he took me with him. Even if I couldn't throw or catch a ball, I could hand him the nails and the tools. He would set up a kerosene heater to ward off the damp coastal chill and we'd spend several hours on the house, him hanging shelves and drywall, me sitting there on bare plywood, two stories up, shivering and writing stories in my head and wishing I could be back in my room with a book.

The teachers at Pace Academy put a lot of emphasis on creative writing, something I'd become rather good at. Most of the stuff I wrote at that age was what we'd now think of as fan fiction: stories that extended or just plain stole from my favorites by Edward Eager and the Alfred Hitchcock and the Three Investigators series. I thought the Hardy Boys books were wooden and repetitive, but I did borrow a bit from cartoons I liked. One day after I read a story inspired by *G-Force* (itself an Americanized update of the Japanese manga *Science Ninja Team Gatchaman*), my classmates applauded. Thunder and lightning went off in my head. *This is what I was put on Earth to do*, I thought, amazed people actually thought I was good at something. It was one thing to diagram sentences and get hundreds on spelling tests, but stories brought people to me instead of pushing them away. Stories got me through those damp mornings on top of the new house, through our endless drives between Greenville and New Bern, through any number of boring classes I could get As in while listening with one ear.

Inclement weather aside, one reason I looked forward to visiting the house was that one of the ducks, a male mallard that had taken up residence in the two ponds, was friendly enough to let me pick him up and walk around with him in my arms. He seemed to have an injury and hadn't migrated with the rest of his flock. Whenever we were there, I'd climb through the undergrowth and low trees at the back of the property (by this point, I'd more or less pounded a trail along the perimeter of the pond) to find him. He was there often enough that the scratches were worth it. Until one day he wasn't.

"Oh, one of the workmen probably saw you walking around with him," Laura suggested when I asked what she thought had happened to him. "Ducks are delicious. He started to trust people. You should have been more careful."

There seemed to be no end to my carelessness, in fact. One afternoon, one of the other Carolina Country Day parents who lived in Brook Valley was dropping us off at the new house. It was close enough to being done that we could go inside. Some days, the Marine and Laura would stop by after work to do things. This day, I closed the car door on Janelle's hand by accident. Her shrieks masked the delicate snap of a bone breaking.

"It's broken! It's broken!"

Mr. Gallagher and a couple of the workmen clustered

around us. The finger was already swelling, and Janelle was sobbing.

"Oh, it's nothing," Laura said. "We'll put some ice on it."

"I think you better take your little girl to the hospital," one of the workmen said.

"I *think*," Laura snapped, "you better do your goddamn *job*."

There was no ice in the new house and no trip to the hospital. Laura gave Janelle a couple of aspirin, and Janelle learned a few things about pain. Her friends at school told their parents about the broken-finger incident. Laura and the Marine were too busy with the new house and their own concerns to notice how many of the other parents stopped speaking to them. As far as I know, they didn't even make the connection when they threw a party later and nobody came.

After weeks or months of delays and clammy, duckless weekends, we moved in. The excitement of living in our modern mansion kept us—or kept me, at least—from noticing how much of the place wasn't finished yet. I'd never lived in a newly built house before and assumed that it was just how things worked: once the walls were up and the roof was on and the lights lit up when you flipped the switch, you moved in and sorted the rest out as time and funds permitted. The local carpet shops only had a few choices available in sizes large enough for our rooms—the colors sane people wouldn't want, in other words, which is how they ended up in our house. There were acres of a bright acid green for the bedrooms, and you could have carpeted Lucifer's living room with the splotchy blue-white-brown combo that we used downstairs. Did it matter, though? The tall windows cranked open and shut instead of sliding up and down. The whole house felt airy and light, unlike most of the homes we had lived in or visited. The architectural vernacular of eastern North Carolina emphasizes doilies, dark wood, and dimness at the expense of basics like sunlight and air. The Marine and Laura proudly said the woodstove, a postmodern black hemicylinder that heated the whole house that first winter, was the only one of its kind east of the Mississippi; they had ordered it from some company in Colorado. Thick insulation and shade from the trees meant we would rarely need air conditioning in the summer or the heat pump in the winter. There was that mad, insane playroom up on the top floor with its view out over the treetops. And perhaps best of all, we had a pond!

Never mind that we were two kids who couldn't swim (the Marine once let me sink to the bottom of a swimming pool to rescue Janelle when she jumped in by herself), we still couldn't wait to get into the water.

"It's filthy," Laura insisted. "You wouldn't believe what people throw in there."

"But… don't fish live in it? And turtles? We've seen them. It can't be that bad."

"I was walking across the bridge between our pond and the one on the golf course one time after a big rainstorm, and I saw something floating. I thought it was a piece of wood at first, but you know what it was?" She lowered her voice to a stage whisper: "It was a *sex toy*."

This is how I actually learned what a dildo was. Laura recounted the tale in tones of exaggerated, giggling horror: *Bigger than life-size! Covered in slime! Only the filthiest people imaginable would use something like that!* There had been some earlier discussion of dildos and vibrators when the Marine and Laura had been called upon to get rid of my Uncle Rudy's sex paraphernalia, but as was often the case with me, I didn't make the connection until later, much less come to understand why someone might want to stick one up his ass. Especially the kind of dick-shaped yule log Laura claimed to have seen in the water. Kids that age probably ought not to have their heads filled with images of buttholes stretched to the snapping point by enormous fake plastic dongs, but then, we weren't exactly a normal family.

The first of the two times I ended up in the pond—the time it was voluntary—happened when the Marine and Laura finally relented, when Janelle and I finally wore them down. We could go in, they said, but on one condition: we couldn't go back into the house before rinsing ourselves off completely with the garden hose, and we had to leave our polluted swimsuits on the landing of the stairs that came up from the basement. Laura didn't want us dripping pond scum on the carpets. That this would entail dashing naked through the house and up a flight of stairs didn't occur to us; still too young to find this request at all weird, we said yes, put on our bathing suits, and raced down the sloping lawn to the pond. At the edge (I hesitate to call it a shore), we hesitated. The trunk of a fallen tree demarcated the border of that part the lawn. The stream that fed the pond formed the rest of that border. We owned the land on the other side as well, but there was nothing over there but a patch of bare ground and some woods. Lacking a pier like the one at our uncle Brian and aunt Vanessa's (Brian was Granny's brother; Vanessa, his irritating wife who punctuated literally every sentence with a giggle) river house, where we spent the occasional weekend, we just had to wade right in.

"Yuck," said Janelle, who went first.

The sandy, algal muck that formed the bed of the pond

squished between our toes. With each step, we sank in almost to our ankles. I consoled myself that at least here, we wouldn't have to worry about stepping on clamshells and crabs. No barnacles to scrape our knees and shins, either. (I still cannot stand the sight of them.) Squelch squelch squelch, and we were almost in the middle. It wasn't even deep, only four or five feet in the center. Why we weren't terrified of quicksand or snakes, I don't know. For about twenty minutes, we tried to play for the sake of playing: we felt obliged to enjoy ourselves, and tried. It didn't last long because we were too grossed out to endure it any longer. On dry land, we looked like we'd been dipped in diarrhea.

Laura's face said *Are you happy now?*, but for once her mouth remained shut.

We hosed off; Janelle rushed upstairs first to bathe in the bathroom we had once shared, and once she was safely out of view, I followed, taking a shower in the bathroom that it was increasingly obvious Granny was never going to use. As the brown sludge sluiced away, I wondered why we had ever bothered. We couldn't swim. The pond was nasty.

From somewhere came the decision that Janelle and I had to have swimming lessons. A few weeks after the school year at Carolina Country Day (which had changed its name from Pace Academy) wrapped up, we were to begin taking lessons at Raynez, a business run by a local family with a reputation for being mean. Anxious, unsure what to expect, we rode our bikes there for our first day of lessons. Would the Raynezes yell at us for being lousy swimmers? Would they hit us or tape our mouths shut and put us in a locker if we weren't any good? Would we drown? Less than a mile from where we lived, the swim school was located at the end of a long driveway that led back into the pines. There was something idyllic in this: hot clear early-summer days in the South, diamonds of sunlight through the trees, a cold pool to splash around in. Better yet, nobody seemed particularly mean, just old and tanned to leather from years in the sun and a bit gruff in the way of adults who smoke a lot between lessons.

I turned out to have a bit of a knack for it, which is to say that as long as I had goggles on (I have a phobia about anything touching my eyes), I was unlikely to drown. At least not immediately. The two weeks of our lessons passed quickly enough, and a few days after we finished, by which time I could thrash my way from one end of the pool to the other, the Marine announced that we would be going for tryouts.

"For what?"

He rustled the newspaper.

"The Greenville Swim Club."

There was no point in offering a rejoinder like "But what if we don't want to?" because we didn't have any say in the matter. A couple of evenings later, we put our swimsuits on under our clothes and piled into the car. The Marine and Laura drove us to Minges Coliseum, the athletic facility next to the ECU football stadium. Without knowing much about what we were supposed to do, we followed them into the natatorium, registered, stripped down to our swimsuits, waited our turn, got into the pool, and dutifully swam from one end to the other. Afterward, we were told which teams we'd been assigned to: I was on the C Team, and Janelle was in the group for little kids who could sort of swim and whose parents wanted them out of the house at the same time of night as their older siblings.

About a week later, the routine that would shape my next five years began. A small Speedo replaced my generic swim trunks. I'd never worn one before. It felt like a couple of strips of duct tape covering my butt and my junk. Since most of my extracurricular experiences with tape had involved Laura sealing my mouth shut with it, this was not a sensation I liked very much. It didn't leave much to the imagination, either. At least with a regular swimsuit, you didn't feel quite so naked, and as I got older and began to develop in various ways, there was never a moment when I didn't feel embarrassed and conspicuous.

Around 6pm, our carpool would arrive to pick us up. Three other kids—including one whose dad had been killed at the same intersection where our own car wreck happened—in our neighborhood had also been chosen, so we'd be riding to practice together. At the pool, we'd put our stuff in lockers, rinse off in the showers, and file out to our respective sections of the natatorium to stretch and start practice. Afterward, we would pass around the Gator Glop, a squeeze bottle containing a mixture of vinegar and rubbing alcohol. The idea was to lean far to one side, squirt some into one ear so that you wouldn't get an infection, let it stay in there for a few seconds, then bend over the other way so that the Gator Glop could run back out. You then repeated the procedure on the opposite side. My head smelled like vinegar and isopropanol for the next five years, but I only got a few ear infections.

Swimming is great when you can reflexively vanish deep into your own head. Having never felt 100% real in the first place, I was practically born for it, or at least retrofitted. The body was there but the mind was not, like when we were driving and Laura would talk nonstop about her work miseries. She didn't seem to have any friends, her new boss was an abusive martinet, and she would describe his tendency to treat her as if she had the IQ of a thumbtack in grinding detail. How he contradicted his instructions and berated her for not being able to track with the changes. How she developed the habit of logging everything he said in order to confront him with it when he stopped making sense. How she had to go to the ladies' room at least once a day to cry in a stall because of his constant, petty insults. If we were on our way to New Bern to see Granny, Janelle would be sitting in the back seat bumping herself into a numbness. Somehow Laura had grown used to driving with that distraction. As for me, I had no choice but to sit there and slip into my own version of nonexistence while she ranted, grunting now and then and resurfacing just enough to listen for something I could respond to, offer a couple of words to make it seem as if I was paying attention, then disappearing again. Thus equipped, I was a natural at distance freestyle. I wouldn't say I loved it, exactly, I never found it boring either. To be bored, you have to be present. I wasn't.

In the locker room, things got more complicated. I didn't want to be naked in front of the other boys. It brought back hideous memories of the Marine's decision to send me to athletic camp one summer. He really didn't explain what it was or why I was going, only that I was.

"But I'm not a jock!" I protested, knowing I'd be overruled.

He glowered at me, his signature look that threatened violence. There was no point in arguing. He'd just belt me. I sulked in the car on the way to Minges Coliseum, the same place where years later I would have swim practice sometimes twice a day, morning and night. He brought me inside to register me for the camp.

It was like PE class, but it went on all day. It was basically my idea of hell.

Basketball? Forget it. *You throw like a girl,* I was told. Like I'd never heard *that* one before. I lacked the coordination to run and dribble. At best, I had about a 10% chance of making the ball go through the netted hoop, and I'm being generous in retrospect. Baseball and softball? Again, the utter lack of coordination killed my chances for success. I had no sense of where the ball would go after the pitcher threw it, nor of where to swing the bat and how hard. Soccer? For that, you have to be able to run for a long time, which I couldn't, not without getting a painful stitch in my side, and you're not supposed to wear sandals. Being told *You run like you've just been fucked up the ass* at least once a day doesn't help. Then there was the whole changing-room thing afterward.

"Can I go somewhere else and do this?" I asked one of the camp staff, terrified.

This attracted attention. Jeering commenced.

"Why?" asked the staff guy.

Because I'm about to die of embarrassment? Because my father has made fun of my body all my life, starting from when I was five years old and got a hard-on in the shower at the gym he dragged me to, during one of his exercise phases? Because I'm ashamed of myself?

I scrambled for something, anything that would get my desperation across. "Because I'm very modest?"

"MODESTY! MODESTY!" screamed every boy in earshot. "MODESTY!"

I endured about two more days of this, each worse than the next as the MODESTY nickname spread. Even the camp counselors started calling me that.

My school friend Timmy Cohen was also there. He liked the camp no better than I did, but he'd mastered the trick of becoming invisible better than I had. When I asked him about changing out of his swimsuit, he said he'd just ducked into one of the bathroom stalls for that.

"Didn't you have to ask?"

"Why would you ask? I just did it."

Now that I was on the swim team with no end in sight (I lasted about three days at the athletic camp and finally convinced Laura to withdraw me), I tried Timmy's bathroom-stall trick when I had to change out of my Speedo after practice. I didn't know which was worse, though: the likelihood of stepping in other guys' piss puddles or the annihilating awfulness of nudity. When it occurred to me that if I put my shirt on first, it would sort of cover things up around front, the toilet stall became a lot less appealing. Boys miss commodes but mostly don't look at dicks. There were exceptions. One little Japanese kid named Satoshi was utterly uninhibited and would climb up onto one of the locker-room benches to dance around. He thought it was hilarious to make his tiny little penis bob up and down. The rest of the boys called it "french-fry dancing" when he did this and would howl with laughter. A couple of the older ones weren't shy at all and calmly walked around in the nude after hitting the showers. As for me, I spent every second in the locker room in a taut state of hyperawareness: trying not to be noticed, trying not to see the other boys naked, wanting to see the other boys naked, wanting to not want to see the other boys naked, refusing to parse any of this on any conscious level, stifling all such thoughts completely, trying not to attract any attention at all, and glancing at their dicks anyway.

For my first swim meet, which was in Wilmington, sometime during that first year on the swim team, we left from Granny's trailer in New Bern. On some level I understood that this would be some sort of race or competition, but the full weight of it didn't hit me until we got in the car and started driving south. It was five in the morning. I was eleven years old. I think this was the first time I had felt the unique and slightly gorgeous loneliness of travel: the world was beautiful in the bluish dark before sunrise. The tall pine trees in the lot creaked in night-time breezes coming off the nearby Neuse River. The Marine stopped at a McDonald's on the way out of New Bern to pick up breakfast. The headlights of his little Datsun hatchback turned the reflective squares on the painted median line into a string of glowing jewels. The night sky was just beginning its fade from black to blue, with traces of greyish light off to the east. The road was deserted, and the Marine sped south. Donna Summer's "The Wanderer" came on the radio. I had one knot in my stomach and another in my throat. The Marine and I didn't really talk: he drove; I ate, and worried.

Somewhere outside of Wilmington, breakfast abruptly disagreed with me. I rolled down the window but puked before I could get my head all the way out.

"Oh *fuck*," the Marine said.

He pulled over and we cleaned up the mess as best we could with fast-food napkins. The car smelled like puke, so we had to drive with the windows down. The feeling of shame and frustration was bad enough, but the sadness intensified it. I already knew I couldn't trust my body. I didn't throw up much, but I knew my digestive system couldn't be relied upon to do its job without pain and messiness. I was nervous. I had what Laura called a "nervous stomach" (which would later be diagnosed as IBS) and always had to go to the bathroom when my anxiety spiked. Always being chosen last for teams gives you negative momentum. You don't want to compete. There's already an expectation you'll be clumsy, fuck things up for everyone else, and be berated or beaten up for it. Nobody had said that I swam like I had a dick up my ass, at least. This was an improvement over running, over every other sport I'd been forced to try, but I'd never been keen on the whole swim team thing to begin with. I was only doing it because the Marine had finally gotten his way, finally forced me into some kind of sport, and while I didn't hate it, I just stayed blanked out more and more of the time. But when breakfast comes up and your father has that disgusted look on his face, the look you've been seeing all your life, the nausea and the mess block your mental getaway. You can't check out and skip the experience.

We found the UNC-Wilmington campus without much trouble, parked, found the natatorium, found the other members of my swim team waiting around on beach towels for their events. No one told me you spent most of your time at swim meets waiting. Even with a book, I was bored, I was nauseated, and I have absolutely no recollection of swimming that day. I was in one of the slower heats since I could barely swim. The older boys and girls who sliced through the water like torpedoes—they amazed me. I never thought I might become like them. My body was too wormy and uncoordinated. I have no idea how I placed that day. Near the bottom, probably. I didn't even get a ribbon for winning the heat, and I dreaded going home afterward. As she always did, Laura would squeal "I'm so *proud* of you!" (over time, I came to think she'd read it in a parenting manual: you were supposed to praise your kids often by telling them you were proud of them so that they'd feel valued and turn out well-adjusted) while continuing to act the opposite. The Marine did this too, just not as effusively.

As time went on, I came to enjoy swim meets, or at least

tolerate them once the vomiting and diarrhea subsided. Although no power on Earth could make me strip off my swimsuit in the locker room afterward (I showered with my suit on and continued to put on my shirt first so that nobody would see me naked), I began to like competing. Somewhere along the way, I turned out to be pretty fast. I started winning.

I didn't always win the 100 freestyle. I was more likely to come in 3rd. My events were the 200 and the 500. Sometimes the 800 or the 1000. At meets, I would sign up for these and usually win them. No one else had the endurance, or if they did, they chose not to use it. Most other swimmers were sprinters. I rarely bothered signing up for the 50: quite a few of the boys were a lot faster off the block than I was. I needed longer to build up my momentum, but once I had, I could maintain it longer; I could just keep going. Besides, I had an advantage. Since I wasn't actually there, it was easy.

CHAPTER 7: HOW TO BE A HUMAN

The night before I was to start the seventh grade, I picked at dinner. I don't remember what Laura cooked, only that I couldn't force much of it down. After six years in the Carolina Country Day safety bubble, surrounded only by other upper-middle-class white kids, I had a head full of horror fantasies about what the coming days would involve. Having parents who didn't socialize meant I hadn't met many kids from public school. I imagined knife gangs and bullies who'd steal my lunch money, shove my head in the toilet, and pee on my legs as I flailed to escape. The idea of eating a school lunch... one CCD classmate (who shall remain nameless) insisted the cafeteria workers routinely spat in the soup. *Always flush twice if you take a shit*, went the conventional wisdom. *It's a long way to the cafeteria*. Besides, I had a solid six-year foundation of intellectual snobbery to support me. After all, Janelle and I had been sent to Pace/CCD because we were *so intelligent*.

It might not have been a recipe for disaster, but the ingredients for a stew of extreme discomfort were all lined up on the kitchen counter. Janelle did well enough at her own school—she at least had the benefit of some social skills—but I was awkward and stiff. Think of the dorky main character in the film *Napoleon Dynamite*. I talked like him too, albeit with a gayish layer of Southern drawl drizzled over the top. I even looked like him. Younger, of course, but there were enough similarities to things I'd prefer to forget that I couldn't enjoy that film as much as my friends did. It's not that I was such a little flamer that you could have fried eggs on my ass, or I didn't *think* I was, but did it matter? Everyone else seemed to think so, and the bar was set low. If any gayish traits manifested at all or even lurked below the surface, other kids would sense the difference, single you out, and call you a faggot. It doesn't take much. Just a whiff of it on top of any other trait that made you stand out in some way guaranteed your life would be hell. I didn't even know what the word meant until I'd been called one nonstop for a couple of weeks. It wasn't in the dictionary, but I did find "ego-dystonic homosexuality" in our medical encyclopedia at home.

It seems funny in retrospect: the Marine and Laura never simply sat down and talked with me about the behaviors they found effeminate or distasteful, like the phase where I wore one of those koala-bear clip things on my collar, and too much jewelry. Yes, I outgrew that, but in the meantime, the disdain from all directions was like mortar fire. Under bombardment without quite grasping why or what to do about it, I seemed powerless to stop disgusting everyone around me. Now and then the Marine would explode and beat the crap out of me, way out of proportion to whatever I'd done; and those belt-lashings always seemed to be more about his own pent-up rage and revulsion than actual discipline. Another pattern was also emerging: sometimes it seemed Laura was encouraging him to do it later so that (a) she could comfort me later and (b) tell me how horrible being *like that* was, and she was sure I wasn't *like that.* So I began living simultaneously in parallel universes. On the one hand, I got straight As without having to try. On the first day of seventh-grade English class, the teacher gave all the students a placement test. I finished it in about ten minutes. When I walked to the back of the room to give it to her, Mrs. Avery asked, "Don't you need more time to finish?"

"No," I said, puzzled. "Why would I?"

I got a 100 on it, or close.

One group of students scored higher on the test than the rest, or so we were told. The white ones. Most of the kids in that class were black. Mrs. Adams therefore set up a separate mini-class and gave us our own self-paced lessons. This didn't seem fair. I wondered: *Not one of the black kids scored well on that test? And all of the white ones actually did?* I didn't buy it then and never have, but there was no one I could say these things to. I came to like that class very much: it was different and fun. There was creativity. I could write. Mostly we were left alone. The layout of the school made this possible: it was divided into four "pods" made up of two pairs of terrible open classrooms each (if one of the teachers had a booming voice, the other one was screwed), with a sunken "pit" in the center. There were beanbag chairs, low tables, piles of books. Goofy seventies school architecture at its best. During English class, the seven of us retreated to the pit to do whatever our assignments were and kind of hang out. In today's world, such overt racism would result in a lawsuit or three, with scalding editorials in the local paper, Twitter seething, and think pieces in the *Huffington Post, Salon,* and a few on Medium. Back then, in eastern North Carolina at the dawn of the 1980s, the world had not begun to move on.

Within a few weeks of meeting my math teacher for the first time that fall, I managed to make him detest me. I turned in my first test of the year. In a patronizing tone, he said, "Let's put our last names on it, shall we?" For six years, I'd only written Marshall in the top right corner of my papers when I handed them in. How many Marshalls were there, after all? But that tone of voice is a button for me, and apparently has been ever since I clawed my way out of the womb. The teacher pushed it and I pushed back:

"It would look kind of funny with Marshall Moore-Wilson on it, wouldn't it? Since that's not my name?"

He sucked in his breath through his teeth and tried to incinerate me with his gaze. He ran the school's Gifted & Talented program, too. Students who placed into it were exempted from one science and one math class every week to attend G&T, as we called it. (Being older, I have come to prefer a different G&T, the kind that involves ice and a lime wedge.) We'd do science experiments, go on field trips, and do other academic-enrichment things. The day I couldn't bear to watch Mr. Wilson's pet snake eat a mouse, a spectacle I still don't know how we were supposed to benefit from (it was the South, after all; there was no lack of roadkill), he gave me the same glare of disgust the Marine often did. I'd discovered my superpower.

In a small private school like Carolina Country Day, difference is tolerated because everybody knows everybody. You've grown up together. Ostracism is unworkable: with less than fifteen students in the entire sixth grade, most of whom have been in school together for years, a certain dynamic emerges. Even my childhood nemesis Julian and I reached a sort of détente (and are now on good terms as adults). The other students made room for my quirks because many of them had their own. The older I got, the more of an outlier I became, but there was still space on the graph for my big purple dot. When

I transferred to Greenville Middle School, though, the much larger number of students—several hundred—increased the pressure to conform.

The Marine and Laura meant well in their own damaged ways but were not of much help. After a day of name-calling and being pushed down on the athletic field and spat upon during PE, sometimes all three if the teacher didn't put a stop to it first, I'd curl up in my room with a book. I had taken over the big bedroom intended for Granny and turned the larger of the two closets into a reading room. I put my beanbag chair in there and covered it with my sleeping bag. That closet was the safest place to be. I would remain there as long as I could. Laura tried to console me with comments like *They're just afraid of you because you're so smart* and, even stranger, *They're scared to get in a fight with you because... you've got long arms.* Even back then, as clueless as I was, this made not the first shred of sense. This one did, though: *It's okay, honey. I know you're not like that.* The Marine, on the other hand, did nothing, apparently thinking any crap I was getting at school would toughen me up. Since he also seemed to think he could beat the sissy-dorkness out of me, the lack of concern came as no real surprise.

As time passed, I began to realize I was seen as a freak, and perhaps not without reason. The stiff, self-conscious gait when I walked that turned into a sort of propulsive but strangely girlish lurch when I ran; the weird, nasal laughter that was half hoot and half guffaw; the propensity to mutter to myself since few others wanted to talk to me... it went beyond quirks and eccentricity. Today, I'd probably be diagnosed with something on the spectrum, medicated, and sent to a counselor or a social worker a couple of times a week.

One day, in music class, three of the nicer girls decided they needed to have a talk with me: "Look, Marshall, about your laugh." They tried to demonstrate it. The first flash of shame burned off quickly when I saw they were sincere. We ignored Mr. Johnson—the music teacher—and his vain and doomed attempts to rally the students around rehearsals for a musical. I had not yet missed a class but it would be a few more months before I realized he intended to put on some sort of play, starring us. Like so much else, this had not been explained. Mercifully, swim practice exempted me from a great many such public discomforts. We formed a tight circle on the floor and talked with the intensity of middle school students impressed with themselves for having noticed that the world no longer seems new.

"And the way you talk... you don't need to drag out every other word. Where are you from, anyway?"

They didn't believe I had grown up in Greenville and New Bern, just forty-five minutes down the road. At the time, I lacked the vernacular to explain the hybrid accent I'd grown up with: Outer Banks High Tide by way of Coonass, Louisiana.

Another girl overheard and remarked, "Oh good, so you're teaching him how to be a human!" The line has stayed with me every day of my life: not cruel, just sharply accurate.

I was disappointed when no further lessons were offered. I even asked for more. Maybe they thought I'd been a lousy pupil. Maybe nothing had changed. I'm not sure anything they told me really helped—although I compressed my laugh into something less feral and began paying attention to the way I stressed certain words when I talked, preemptively flattening out syllables to keep from exaggerating them—but I was glad they made the effort. No one else had, or would. It was going to be up to me.

If you try hard enough, the Marine insisted, you can accomplish anything with your mind. He and Laura both claimed the '60s had been silly, all that LSD and the flower children who took it, all the rebellion and psychedelia, but they were products of it nonetheless. A great many of the books in the house were about the occult. We had a Ouija board and Zener cards. If you put your mind to it, then... you could be telekinetic. You could do anything. All that parapsychology research in the late '60s proved it, or so I came to believe. I read everything in the house on the subject and checked out more at the library: ghosts, reincarnation, telekinesis, telepathy, clairvoyance, the whole lot. These things could be measured and understood. Scientists were working on it. Following that logic, I assumed I could make myself die without actually having to do something messy and painful like shooting myself or cutting my wrists or hanging myself. Anything's possible if you put your mind to it, after all.

Every night for the rest of that year, or at least most nights, as I lay in bed waiting to fall asleep, I concentrated on not waking up in the morning. Being seen as a human didn't seem to be working out, so perhaps I ought to get rid of myself. It would be better for everyone concerned. To that end, I ground my teeth and probably gave myself early-stage TMJ from concentrating as hard as I could. Psychic people in movies like *Escape to Witch Mountain* activated their powers by frowning, so I frowned ferociously in the dark and tried to be psychic. I tried to pull my soul out of my body, thinking I would be better off elsewhere. Anywhere else, anything else, just not another day with the fucking cretin rednecks I had to go to school with every day. And although I was years away from realizing it, the constant self-monitoring had already worn me out. The way I spoke. The way I walked. The way I moved my hands. The way I'd forget to unclench. (I still forget.) Why fear the afterlife when I was already in hell?

Despite my best efforts, it kept not happening. I woke up every morning and went to school with a lead weight of resignation in my guts. The cumulative exhaustion of vigilance was giving me headaches: trying to avoid the kids who taunted me; updating my mental inventory of safe places I could duck into on a moment's notice; keeping a running tally of the teachers who seemed sympathetic and might intervene.

When Laura said it was important to be able to look into the mirror and say "Self, I love you" every day, I couldn't imagine doing that. For one thing, I couldn't imagine looking into the mirror that long. I despised the way I looked and basically everything about myself. What's the use in being smart if you're such a shambling misfit that everyone you know wants to set you on fire and cheer as you burn? To the extent that there was a ray of light throughout all this, it was that I continued to suspect I wasn't real. None of this was. Somewhere along the way I began to notice little moments I called *surfacing*: I'd experience a tiny jolt of reality—*I exist, and this is happening to me right now!* Sometimes these little jolts back into the real world were enjoyable: eating a big meal of fried shrimp at the Dixie Queen, our favorite restaurant over in neighboring Winterville, or cutting a couple of seconds off my previous time at a swim meet. Other times, it could be something as mundane as taking a dump. Then the daily stress and terror would grind my self-awareness back into hibernation, wherever it went when I wasn't looking.

The idea of not existing after death didn't frighten me because I didn't believe it. Not with all those ghost stories hovering at the edge of my consciousness, not after hearing them all my life. If I could separate myself from my body, I could vanish into the light recounted in so many near-death-experience stories. I could hang out with ghosts, who had to be more interesting than the living, and who probably wouldn't say I walked like I had a dick in my ass or honked through my nose instead of talking. And if not, then existing as a discorporeal entity couldn't possibly be worse than having a body that kept not living up to everyone's expectations in literally every situation other than swimming. (Oh, and the hair. Having a big shock of curly blond hair is great if and only if you spend all your time with old ladies and nobody else.) I couldn't run without pounding my flat feet on the pavement, getting a stitch in my side, and being told I ran like a girl. I couldn't trust my digestive system and was always having to go to the bathroom. Dull, grinding headaches were another constant. I didn't want to kill myself with one of the guns in the house because I was afraid I'd fuck up and live. Being a pariah at school and an awkward source of revulsion to pretty much everyone was bad enough, but what if I ended up lingering at the edge of death, a vegetable, unable to care for myself? That idea more than anything else probably kept me alive during middle school, despite how little I wanted to go on living.

The ABC television miniseries *The Day After* changed my life and perhaps shocked me out of my morbid better-off-dead mindset once and for all. The show aired in 1983. In the story, hostilities had erupted between the Soviet Union and the United States, and various residents of a small Kansas town had to cope with the aftermath of nuclear Armageddon. The Marine and Laura let Janelle and me watch this sort of thing more because they wanted to hear themselves Imparting Wisdom afterward than out of any intrinsic educational value the show might have had. The televised mushroom clouds seared a sense of impending doom across the back of my mind, and the front. Although we all lived with the constant fear that the Russians really might drop the bomb someday, I didn't think humankind would sink to that depth of stupidity. Even so, watching the destruction and its aftermath play out on TV scared the hell out of me. The fireball burnt out one character's eyes, and the young man spent the rest of the film with ragged bandages wrapped around his head; radiation sickness caused a young woman character to grow ill and to bleed from her privates. Some days, the world really did seem to be spinning toward this gruesome end, one in which we would all die shivering and puking and shitting ourselves in fallout shelters. The idea of spending my last choking, diarrhea-plagued moments in the basement with my parents and my sister made me long for the cleansing white fire of Ground Zero. Better a quick flaming death than to have to hear Laura ask if my pubes were growing in funny now that I'd been zapped with radiation.

"What would we do, if that really happened? What would you and Dad do?" I asked her after the credits rolled and mankind's doom was sealed.

"We talked it over, and what we decided was this. Even if we survived the blast, if we weren't in the area that was bombed, we don't think life would be good afterward. There would be no government, no law and order, no food. What we decided was that we'd wait for you and your sister to go to bed one night. Then we'd take one of the guns, and while you were sleeping, we'd shoot you both. Whichever one of us did it would shoot the other, and would then commit suicide. It would be better that way. That way, we would die together as a family. It would be better than living in a world like that, and better than dying separately, one at a time."

I already knew she had been in the habit of knocking Janelle and me out with cough syrup when we were little, not because we were sick but to give herself the night off. She'd admitted it. Now this: a whole new level of crazy, even for her. To this day, I still cannot hear the words *together as a family* without my skin crawling. But it did quell my obsession with dying in bed.

CHAPTER 8: THE FAMILY ARCANA

Since I rarely saw the inside of other people's homes, I had to fill in a lot of blanks about how people lived, how families interacted. For example, I assumed everybody had a Ouija board in the storage closet down the hall, just as they must also have a gun rack in the master bedroom plus a couple of pistols in various strategic locations around the house. Like the Foxfire survivalist books on the shelves next to the ones by Nostradamus and Edgar Cayce, the cord and a half of firewood stacked up in the backyard and the basement, the pharmacy in the purse to ward off unwanted emotions and physical sensations, and the fourth car (a vast beige barge of a Mercury Marquis sedan), supplies for all possible contingencies were just... how things were done. You had to be prepared for every eventuality: shooting burglars in the middle of the night, anesthetizing the horrors away as you mopped up the blood, and contacting their departed souls afterward to ask them to stop throwing the china and cutlery around the room.

It also never occurred to me that other people's parents weren't psychic.

"I know everything you're thinking," Laura said once, when I was still very young.

Worried, I asked, "You do?" I tended to worry because I had begun to notice that people liked to trick me. Lacking the bullshit filter everyone else seemed to have, I took everything literally and tended to believe people, even the ones whose past shenanigans should have been big red warning flags about imminent lies.

Laura nodded gravely. "Yes. Sometimes your father and I communicate that way. I think about him, and he calls me. If I need him to pick up something from the store after work, I think about it. Sometimes he knows, and he does it for me. We have a very special bond. Just like you and I do."

These discussions would often lead into deeper into the family arcana, right up to the militarized borders of the Things We Weren't Supposed to Talk About:

"When your father's plane was sabotaged, I *knew* it. Someone put ball bearings in his fuel tank. He had to bail out. His parachute malfunctioned, too. It didn't open until it was almost too late. It's a miracle he wasn't killed! And I *knew*, even before the phone call came, that something bad had happened to him, but he'd survived. He was going to be okay."

Per the no-questions-about-Vietnam rule, I could never ask what he'd done and whom he'd pissed off. (I still have no idea.)

She always returned to her ghost stories, though, for there can be no Southern without a generous helping of Gothic. When Laura's father (Dick) passed away, he returned a few days after the funeral as a cloud of haze that smelled like his pipe smoke. This cloud would appear in the stairwell in the Johnson Street house in New Bern. The Little Red House on Johnson Street, as she called it. Laura said that, far from being frightened of these apparitions, she liked to stand in them. Although I find it hard to imagine wanting to live in a house that smelled like Dick, she said these manifestations were comforting. (I used a version of this story in my novel *Inhospitable*.)

Granny also got in on the ghost-story action every chance she got: "The night I brought William [Laura's baby brother, who died in his crib] home from the hospital, I knew he wasn't gonna make it. Something woke me up in the night. I saw my mother standing at the foot of my bed, crying." Two other deceased women relatives appeared next to her as well; all were crying. Nothing was said, but Granny understood they had come for William. He had the autoimmune blood disorder now known as HDN, hemolytic disease of the newborn. Basically, he was allergic to himself. At the time, there was no treatment; he had no hope of surviving through the night. "I wasn't scared," Granny went on. "Just sad, and tired. I knew why they had come."

This was the fabric of my reality.

Jewel, the Marine's mother, had been killed in a car wreck. She and her husband (his father) been driving home one night on a deserted road. Something happened and they lost control of the car. Patrick was thrown clear, but Jewel's seatbelt locked. She couldn't free herself, and when the car caught fire, she burned to death.

"The night it happened," Laura said, "I woke up in a cold sweat. It was like somebody had wrapped me in a cold wet grey sheet. I was cold all over. My teeth were chattering, and I couldn't get warm. And that's when the call came. When the phone rang, your father gave me a look. I told him, 'It's about your mother. Something's happened to your mother.' He answered the phone, and he went white as a sheet. His mother had just been killed, all right, and I knew. I *knew*."

The first time I heard this story, I asked, "Didn't she have nail scissors in her purse? You do. Couldn't she have cut through the seatbelt, if it wouldn't unlatch?"

"She was knocked out," Laura insisted, but a note of—something?—in her voice hinted that she didn't entirely believe the story she was telling. "She was unconscious. So was your grandfather. Don't ask more questions. I wasn't there when it happened."

"But you *knew*. You woke up in the middle of the night, before the phone rang."

"Be that as it may."

The weird stories, which I liked, continued well into my teens. So did her claims of telepathic monitoring, which I was considerably less fond of. (In retrospect, I have wondered if she was just trying to keep me from jerking off. She didn't succeed.) As a result, well, to say that I became uncomfortable around my mother would be like saying the air on Venus might be a bit difficult to breathe. For one thing, there was her nutty insistence that she *owned* us and we were still under warranty. On her bad days, the ones when she wasn't tearfully threatening to pack all of her shit in her station wagon and drive away, never to see any of us again, she'd scream, "I gave birth to you! I gave you life! I can take it away!" She also had odd ideas about hygiene, insisting on inspecting Janelle's vagina and cleaning it with Q-tips often enough that I just assumed this was what vaginas required, that it was some kind of lady-maintenance thing. Periods and whatnot. Better not to ask.

"Don't forget to wash under your foreskin!" Laura would sometimes call when I went to take a shower. This confused me for years. I am circumcised. And she had an icky, bizarre fascination with popping our zits. I think it must be a Southern-women thing: when I read Armistead Maupin's memoir

Logical Family not long ago, I was both relieved and revolted to discover his mother did that too, squeezing the pus out of visible blemishes and holding up a fingernail to show off the bloody effluent. Besides, the whole "we talked about killing you in your sleep" thing was never far from my mind. I was trapped in some kind of bad carnival. Something wicked this way had long since come, unlocked the door, let itself in, unpacked its shit, and settled in for a long stay. There was no escape, not for several more years anyway.

Then there was the night of the prowler. The Marine was away on a business trip. Now and then that happened: he had to go to Atlanta and Dallas for work. When I got a bit older, I noticed he kept condoms at home and would take them on these trips. That night, which was dark and cold but not stormy, the phone rang. Laura answered it, went rigid, set the headset back in its cradle, and told me to lock the door after she went out.

"That was Lisa Zimmerman from next door. She's all alone, and there's a prowler. Someone just came scratching at the windows, trying to get into the house. Don't let anyone else in but me, do you understand?"

Laura ran to her office, got her gun, and charged out of the house.

I figured it was safe enough to go downstairs to the basement. I knew where all The Marine's tools were kept and thought one of the larger hammers would do the most damage, if it came to that. Although there were a few big knives in the kitchen, I figured anyone crazy enough to break in might be expecting that. Knives are predictable but hammers are surprising, especially when an 11-year-old is beating your head in with one.

Janelle was upstairs either in bed or bumping, oblivious either way.

I sat by the door until Laura came home.

"Whoever it was, when they heard me coming, they ran away," she said.

That night, there was a cold snap. Temperatures Down East don't drop below freezing much, but that night, they did. The next morning, a woman was found frozen in a pond in the neighborhood next to ours.

"Don't tell your father," Laura said. "We wouldn't want him to get worried."

As far as I know, no bullet holes were discovered in the body.

This pattern of "don't ask, don't tell" was our norm long before Barney Frank thought up his own version for the US military. Case in point, I definitely ought not to have mentioned getting pubes. This was the event that ended me telling Laura everything that happened with my body. Before that, I didn't hesitate. She was Mom. It was our version of normal. Armpit hair, no big deal. I was on the swim team. She could see it coming in, and remarked upon it several times, cloying statements like "My baby's becoming a man now" she would punctuate with agonized sighs as if every body hair I sprouted brought her a day closer to the grave. "It seems like only yesterday that I was changing your diapers... I remember the first time I changed you, after I brought you home from the hospital. Your little ding-dong stood straight up and you peed in my face! I needed windshield wipers for my glasses!"

There was no avoiding the physical reality: I *was* getting pubes. It was like a couple of years earlier, when the down on my chin had begun to darken and thicken. We were in the car, driving through one of the towns near the inland coast on one of our Sunday-afternoon excursions. Belhaven, Edenton, Bath—I can't remember which one it was now. I usually enjoyed these, as long as I wasn't the center of attention. The Marine tugged at a tuft of my stubble and declared it was time I started shaving.

"Then shouldn't you show him how?" Laura asked.

"You put shaving cream on it, take a razor, and shave it off."

That was more or less the end of that conversation. The next time we went shopping, Laura told me to pick out a can of shaving cream and some razors. Somehow I managed to figure the rest out on my own without slicing off my cheeks and chin.

The Marine's disinclination to show me what to do came as no surprise. On the one hand, he was only too happy to drive me to swim meets or science fairs, the things I was good at and he could take credit for at work the next day. Along the same lines, there was the ongoing issue of my masculinity or lack thereof. By this time, at the onset of my teens, I already knew I was gay: I understood it in the way people know uncomfortable truths about themselves but can only admit them in the dark, late at night, in the raw and honest interval before falling asleep. It's not that I was overtly girlish, exactly, more that the lack of a family social life meant the only male role model around was coarse and boorish and often drunk in his armchair, not like me in any meaningful way, not someone I wanted to emulate or even could. He had the emotional range of a golem, inert much of the time but still exuding an inchoate menace, and now and then rising out of his inanimate stupor and taking on some dark, arcane ab-life when he wanted to inflict damage. To add to the isolation, for most of my life I had attended a very small private school, entirely staffed and run by women. I had no other living male relatives that I knew of, apart from Granny's two brothers and their own families, whom I saw maybe once a year. (Well, I did have a grandfather, but I was still a few years away from figuring it out.) I'd have acted less like the women in my life if there had been more men around whom I didn't visibly disgust.

Going against a spark of better judgment, I told her I'd grown some hair down there.

"Let me see!" Laura squealed.

She paused on the staircase. I took a couple of steps backward, lest she take a proprietary lunge at my crotch.

"I want to see!"

"Umm... no? It's embarrassing."

"*I wanna see, I wanna see, I wanna see!*"

I fled to my bedroom and shut the door.

She sulked all afternoon, refusing to speak to me; instead, she cast long-suffering glances my way the rest of the day. When the Marine got home from work and heard what happened, he snapped, "Christ, Laura. Leave him alone, then."

When he wasn't around, there were subsequent, grabby attempts (*Please, I want to see... please?*), which grossed me out. I got quiet and stayed that way. I didn't know quite how to snap at her yet, but it wasn't far off. Even as alien to myself as I kept most of my feelings, I was getting angry. She clearly didn't want to take no for an answer, and she kept trying.

Despite my accomplishments in the swimming pool, I fundamentally loathed my body. It wasn't just that I distrusted it, after all the digestive near-disasters. (At times I deliberately wore dark pants, fearing sudden bowel accidents. It never happened but there were a few close calls. Considering all the anal-sex jokes I was the butt of, such a thing would have been impossible for me back then. My digestive system was a mess most of the time and it's not as if anyone wanted to fuck me.)

Mistrust doesn't go far enough: I hated the way I looked and basically everything about myself. I was smart, I could swim, and I could write. Oh, and despite being a dork, I was in some strange way also too pretty to be a boy. Where redeeming features were concerned, that was about it. The supposed transition to manhood couldn't come quickly enough to suit me. Sprouting pubes and armpit hair was a good sign; shaving was a good sign, but I had the physique of a pencil. My quads were big from biking everywhere, and the rest of me was kind of willowy-scrawny. I had no musculature anywhere else, despite all the swimming.

My friend Ellie Norris once said she felt like a collection of spare parts. Those words stuck with me: I always felt the same way. Random pieces no one else was using... let's glue 'em together and see how well the result can walk and talk and take emergency dumps. Laura's prurient fascination with my body exacerbated all my doubts. I was beginning to feel used up, like a batch of depleted uranium: useful only in very narrow, specific ways, radiantly toxic, best avoided.

When I wasn't in class or at the pool, I was reading. By the age of 11, I had read everything of interest in the children's section of Sheppard Memorial Library, which was housed in a splendid old house—more of a mansion, really—at the edge of downtown Greenville. The children's library was downstairs. Air-conditioned to near-Antarctic conditions to keep the damp under control, the place had an invitingly tangy scent of book dust and the ink the librarians used when they stamped books in and out. I read every book I could find on ghosts. I discovered Edward Eager's books down there, wonderful stories about magical goings-on, and written with a certain elegant archness that appealed to me very much and later informed my work.

Any kind of series I could find—Alfred Hitchcock and the Three Investigators, the Miss Pickerell books and the Danny Dunn ones, even Enid Blyton's work (which hasn't aged well but I was too young then to know better)—I devoured. One evening, I stopped halfway down the stairs that led to the basement. The last few times I'd been there, I walked around the stacks looking for something new or at least a spine that hadn't caught my eye before. Why not just go up to the adult section instead? How much harder to read could the books actually be?

Climbing the wide flight of stairs at the main entrance, I mulled over author names I'd seen in bookstores. One came to mind right away: Stephen King. Back then, you couldn't walk past a Waldenbooks without seeing stacks of paperbacks with the name KING emblazoned across the covers, often in bright bloody red. I made my way to the K section of the fiction section. There were two or three of his books on the shelf. I picked up *Firestarter* and brought it to the circulation desk to check out.

"Are you sure you're old enough to read that?" cautioned the librarian. "It's scary."

I think I just glared at her. Going to school every day was scary. A book about a pyrokinetic girl more or less my own age? This wasn't literature, it was *nutrition*.

That weekend, we went down to Brian and Vanessa's river cottage down in Aurora, a settlement on the Pamlico River downstream from Little Washington, where they lived. Granny was there, and a couple of other distant relatives stopped by. The late spring weather turned unseasonably cool: clouds rolled in, intermittent rain fell, and the temperature dropped to about 20 degrees below what it should have been. With two bedrooms, one bathroom, and an open living-room-kitchen combo, the little bungalow was cramped. Family weekends like that only worked when most of us were outdoors.

Normally I loved trips down there. There were paddle boats to ride up and down the river, clams to dig up, crabs to catch and steam. Endless swimming in the wide, shallow river, and we didn't have to get out of the water to pee. Brian and Vanessa themselves could be a bit much (he was gruff and she giggled constantly), but from a kid's point of view, the carpet on the floors of the cottage more than compensated. They'd used samples from a carpet shop that was going out of business, or so the story went, meaning the floors were a mad but cheerful crazy quilt of colors and textures.

Since the weather was too clammy for outdoor pursuits, I found a quiet corner and started reading *Firestarter*. I think I finished it in one sitting. Scary? Please, I'd have taken pyrokinesis and a shadowy government agency over the knuckle-dragging shitheads at school any day of the week. Scary was when you were riding your bike to school, the bus passed by, and half the kids in it flocked to the windows on your side so that they could scream names at you and throw spitballs. Scary was the split-second just before a blob of spit hit your face. Scary was when somebody vandalized your bike in the rack at school in full view of the front office, stomping on the rear wheel long and hard enough to bend the bicycle's entire frame, the secretary claimed not to have seen the culprit(s), and something about the set of her jaw and the cold look in her eye told you she was tacitly on the bullies' side, lying. I'd always read for escape, but this was like switching from candy cigarettes to high-grade hash. Why hadn't anybody told me that the adult section had better books (not to mention loads more of them)?

Stephen King, Peter Straub, Dean Koontz, Robert McCammon, and other writers in the horror genre... well, I won't say they kept me alive during those years because that would sound pathetic. I did the actual work. When it became unsafe to walk through downtown during one of those hideous middle-school summers because a group of older boys who hated me and had violence in mind took to hanging out with their bikes waiting for me, the books were something I could disappear into. Most of the time when this happened, I could duck into a dorm on campus and call security to chase them away. They got braver, though, and a couple of times they followed me into the student center, where Laura worked. Again, security would be called; they'd be strong-armed out the door and ordered not to come back. At home, the Marine would fume: "I'll take out a peace bond on them!" And yet, the miasma remained: this was my fault in some oblique, unspoken way. Straighten up and fly right, or this is what you get. Katy bar the door. Since the only other options were killing myself or them, all I could do was make plans to leave.

I didn't need the Ouija board to see the future: I *would* be leaving. Greenville. North Carolina. Possibly America. I'd heard about a special school up in Durham, the North Carolina School of Science and Mathematics. It had been set up five or six years prior, and it was reputed to be the best high school in the country. You had to be extremely academically gifted to get in. I was, so I figured I had a shot. They took only the best juniors each year, about two hundred from around the state, and you lived on campus in dorms. I figured it had to be a heaven and a haven for nerds, the kind of place where kids like me could have conversations without first needing to calibrate our vocabulary in order to avoid dull-normal strangers and distant relatives saying things like, "You may've got yo'self a lotta book-learnin', but you just don't got any *common sense*."

In that exact moment, I knew I was going to apply. I wouldn't have to do any extra work that I wasn't already doing: I was on the Greenville swim team and the Rose High one at the same time, practicing some three and a half hours every day, and still getting straight As. I did well in science fairs and was in a couple of other gifted-kids programs. Of course NCSSM would accept me. It was just going to be a matter of grinding my teeth and getting through the meantime.

But as a safeguard, I asked the Ouija board about it later. I could get the thing to work and wasn't old enough to be scared of it yet. The planchette slid over to Yes even before I could get the question out of my mouth.

CHAPTER 9: PINECREST

Daytime in Down East North Carolina can be an oppressive, sweltering horror: the hazy grey sky bears down, squeezing all the oxygen out of the air. Nights are better: still torrid, but softer, they give you the feeling of moving through some benign liquid when you walk after sunset. Haze lingers at ground level and swirls among low plants. Insects scream. As spring advances toward summer, this sensory overload coupled with the promise of about two and a half months free from the rest of the lunatics in the asylum results in a sort of classical conditioning: hope and a low current of elation as the weather warms, joy amid all that mugginess, then a fast plunge into despair with the first whiff of fall. To this day, the smell of woodsmoke dumps me into a nostalgia-tinged funk. There's something even worse about the pristine blue skies you see only at that time of year: after the wet torpor of summer has departed, that shade of turquoise is the color of heartache. Worst of all is the roar of a Sunday-afternoon football stadium coming over the TV, with hearty, red-blooded specimens of white American maleness bellowing over the din. The sound of football on TV still makes me want to eat a couple of light bulbs and wash them down with lye.

Apart from the occasional afternoon ambush by the juvenile delinquents who'd hang out downtown and chase me back to campus if they saw me, summers were generally kind. There were trips to Atlantic Beach, only an hour and a half away. Laura would take a day off or we'd go on a Saturday. Now and then, either while we were getting ready or were already in the car, she'd tell us about a recurring nightmare of hers, one in which a tidal wave swept us all out to sea. She would gather us up in her arms (she still told this story when we were teenagers) and try to outrun the tsunami. Everybody died. Bored with this story before we were in our double-digit years, we didn't think about onrushing death by inundation at all; we'd spend some time on the sand or running around in the waves, dry off, pile in the car, and on our way back, eat dinner at the Sanitary Seafood Market in nearby Morehead City (I think it's now called the Sanitary Fish Market, or perhaps it always was). Always fried shrimp for me, plus french fries and a big glass of sweetened iced tea, and we'd buy a box of the restaurant's famous salt-water taffy before we left.

For a year or two, while Laura was between jobs, we owned a secondhand store down in New Bern. She would drive down during the week; on Fridays after work, the Marine would pick Janelle and me up from school, and we'd all stay at Granny's place, going back on Sundays. During the summer, we'd stay longer, sometimes a whole week at a time. We'd visit yard sales on Saturdays looking for items we could mark up and resell. I had no head for it whatsoever and made very little money with my own resale items (Janelle, on the other hand, was much savvier and has since done pretty well for herself in the business world), but I did end up buying boxes of books I ended up loving, notably an old edition of L. Frank Baum's *The Wonderful Wizard of Oz* and four or five of its sequels. For what it's worth, I always thought *The Patchwork Girl of Oz* was kind of weird and disturbing, but *Tik-Tok of Oz* was one of the better ones in the series. Yes, swim practice moved from the two pools on campus (it was usually held at Minges, but sometimes at the older pool at Memorial Gym on main campus, which I liked much better because the locker room was cavernous and you accessed the pool area via a spiral staircase) to Greenville's City Pool, which we predictably nicknamed the Shitty Pool. Other than that, though, the mere fact of being mostly left alone meant that summers were pretty idyllic.

Discovering you've become a very good swimmer is an interesting problem to have. Since the Marine and Laura weren't the kind of parents you could talk rationally about future plans and options with, I was on my own. The idea of trying to discuss it with the Marine... well, that would have entailed talking with him. He didn't talk. He sometimes barked. Now and then he'd sort of wax sentimental, talking *at* me as if I were the kind of son who played sports, had buddies, and chased girls. Then he'd sort of snap out of it and look at me, remembering he was talking to the son he actually had, sometimes punctuating his maunderings with a comment like "Your mother and I... are just so *proud* of you," after which he would gaze out the window, perhaps reflecting on whether he'd sounded sincere enough. But when I started winning distance freestyle events, and even turned out to have a pretty decent butterfly, the few conversations we did have took an interesting spin. For the first time, we started talking—actually *talking*—about the Olympics.

I don't know where the idea came from, whether it was mine or somebody else's. Perhaps one of the other swim-team parents brought it up. But I was reliably winning the 200 and 500 free (or the 400, if the pool was the 50-meter kind), and sometimes even the 1000. Often by fairly big margins, too. At the state level, there wasn't much competition: most boys went out for the shorter events. Although the idea of representing the USA in the Olympics—most likely in Seoul in 1988 because I thought I might be too old by the time Barcelona 1992 rolled around—seemed far-fetched, in a way it also didn't. I *was* pretty good. Better than pretty good, possibly capable of greatness if I were willing to work for it. What I lacked in musculature, I made up for in technique and mad stamina. "Deceptively fast," one of the other parents called me once. In other words, I had an excellent stroke and there wasn't enough of me to get in my own way.

Pinecrest is a swim camp run by a private boarding school in Fort Lauderdale. Or perhaps someone else runs it and has a longstanding contract with the school. I never knew much about the school itself, only that quite a few swimmers who went on to join the US Olympic team trained at Pinecrest during the summer. Kelly Barnhill, the captain of both of the teams in Greenville, had been there one summer already. Already fast, he came back formidable, and I wanted what he had. How I brought up the idea of going, I don't recall. I think his parents gave mine a brochure. You could go from two to eight weeks. Kelly would be down there training for eight weeks that year, so he'd be able to keep an eye on me. I couldn't imagine being away for that long, and neither could the Marine or Laura, but we settled on two. Arrangements were made, plane tickets were bought, and the summer between ninth and tenth grades, I went to Florida.

The night before my flight, I couldn't sleep. The idea of changing planes terrified me. In retrospect, this is hilarious, considering where I live now (Hong Kong when this was written, but I've moved to England since then) and how much

I travel (or did, before the pandemic). I suppose when you're blank half the time because it's all that keeps you from frying in your own anxiety, and when your mother openly admits to keeping you and your sister sheltered, naïve, and sometimes drugged in order to preserve your innocence for as long as possible in this corrupt world, you're at increased risk of getting on the wrong jet—or being kidnapped, which is more or less what happened when I landed in Miami.

Piedmont was the only airline that flew out of eastern North Carolina back in the day. In my childhood, I envied kids who had flown different airlines and visited different countries. The kids at Carolina Country Day spoke in blasé tones about Delta, Eastern, Braniff. One girl in my class had taken a bus tour through Europe. I still remember the part of her story about her dozing off and missing Liechtenstein. In contrast, Greenville was an oasis surrounded by seventy-five miles of tobacco, cotton, and corn in every direction, a vast splotch of agricultural sadness only broken up by swamps, streams, and new subdivisions. So I flew Piedmont from Kinston to Charlotte, then wandered around the airport until I found my connecting flight to Miami.

On arrival, I collected my suitcase and wondered what to do next. My instructions were vague: someone from Pinecrest was supposed to meet me in the arrival hall. It didn't occur to me that the man who picked me up wasn't from Pinecrest until several adult passengers got in the van with him. He approached me and asked where I was going.

"Pinecrest," I said. "Swim camp?"

"Okay, come on."

He dropped the other passengers off first, one at a time.

I saw a lot more of Fort Lauderdale than I wanted to.

I began to worry.

The driver's radio hissed and crackled, and I heard his dispatcher ask if he had someone matching my description. He quickly turned down the volume, but said that he did.

"We're almost there," he said.

When he dropped me off at the school, the place was almost deserted. He charged me ten dollars for the ride, which was most of the money I had on me at the time. This infuriated me: by then, I had realized he wasn't from the school. Before long, I got the complete story: when the camp staff showed up to collect me, I was nowhere to be found. In a panic, they called the school. Someone there called my parents, who also panicked. I never found out the precise chain of events, but calls went out to airport shuttle drivers all over Fort Lauderdale and Miami. Had I not turned up, my parents and the Pinecrest people would have started calling police departments. Fortunately the guy was only an opportunistic dickhead and not a murderous pervert. The ride set me back ten bucks but at least the guy didn't rape me and throw me into a canal afterward for the gators to eat.

When a member of the staff showed me to my room, I discovered I wasn't alone. As if everything else that had happened that day weren't enough, the biggest cockroach I'd ever seen darted across the floor when the door opened. Being faster, I stomped it. I still remember the crunch, but what really caught me off guard was the smell: oddly rancid, like the liquid in the bottom of a garbage can that's been out in the sun. Welcome to Florida.

On the phone later, the Marine was furious, spluttering his usual threats about jerking me out of there so fast my teeth would rattle. Laura said this was just his way of being concerned. Suddenly I realized the immensity of the mistake

I had made, and was horrified... that I'd chosen only the two-week option.

My roommate Jimmy Harris was from Valdosta, Georgia, and was everything that I was not: kind of buff, for one thing, and easy in his own skin in a way that I was not. He looked good in his Speedo and out of it and didn't care who saw his butt. He didn't swagger, either. Well-raised young Southern men don't. There's no need for it, for one thing: gender in the South is a fur-lined corset, and as long as it naturally fits you, it feels great. Besides, Southerners see machismo as *common*. I didn't crave that, exactly, but I envied it. It would have simplified things, opened doors. At the same time, I subtly understood it also wouldn't fit. His version of maleness didn't match mine. Nor did I crave *him*. I wasn't old enough to know it yet, but he wasn't my type. I liked him all right—maybe not a blazing genius bookworm, but a nice well-bred Southern boy too polite to pick on his dorky roommate, and a damn good swimmer—but couldn't escape the feeling that he was everything the Marine wanted in a son and didn't get. Fortunately, Jimmy seemed to find me amusing. We didn't have much to talk about, but his easygoing maleness kept the stress level down.

Overall, I liked the facility: I liked the sun, I liked the gardens on campus, I liked the cheerful portulacas (I didn't know what they were called at first, and had to go to the library and look them up when I got home) growing around the water features. The food was all right, edible, although mostly I ate simple ham-and-cheese sandwiches. I managed to make a few friends, too. Misfits always do. We seek each other out and form our own little *us vs. them* societies. Max from Indiana, Greg from Wyoming, Brad from Louisiana. I didn't keep in touch with those guys, but I remember them.

I *hated* the early morning practices, though. We had to get up at six for a brutal workout, several times more strenuous and demanding than the ones in Greenville, even at the height of training season before big meets. Afterward, during the half-hour interval when most students were given a rest period, I was back in the water having my stroke videotaped for later feedback. After that, there was another brief rest period, maybe half an hour. Then, we alternated between aerobics and weight training. Then, a snack. Then, back in the pool to endure another workout. My ears sunburned, cracked, and bled. So did the rest of me. My sunburn had a sunburn. My skin has never been that dark and unless I die in a fire never will be again.

I quickly came to despise the routine, and worse, I wasn't at the same level as the other kids my age, most of whom had been swimming longer and were more dedicated to the sport. This was where I began to see the difference between Olympic athletes and the rest of us. Several members of the US team did in fact train there that summer; I met them, spoke to a few, forgot their names one second after hearing them. It didn't matter because I already knew I didn't belong. The kids my age were relentless. They talked about training in New York and Mission Viejo. They talked about meets on the national level, events and places I'd barely even heard of. Although I was glad my speed and my stroke were improving, I was too goddamn tired all the time to see any value in what I was doing. My doubts were like the constant aches and cramps in my arms and legs. In aerobics, we had to sweat and groan our way through "She Works Hard for the Money" and "Flashdance" over and over again. I came to loathe those songs. ("Flashdance" in particular scandalized me because of the lyrics I misheard as *"In a flash, it takes hold/ Of my hooooooooole…"*) I hated them almost as much as I hated the slogan "No pain, no gain," which everyone there repeated incessantly. A stitch burned in my side almost from the time I finished stretching out for the first morning workout until I fell into bed at night, incoherent from fatigue. Was this what it would be like if I were to try to push through the membrane separating me from them? Constant exhaustion? Spending summers in places like Pinecrest—which after a week, I was finding unpleasantly institutional?

Then there was the whole "everybody thinks I'm a fag" thing. Kelly tried to talk about it with me once, a couple of days after we got there. I was too uptight, he said. Everybody noticed it. It wasn't that I was a bad guy—basically everyone who knew me conceded I was nice enough—but I had this weird, tightly wrapped persistence. I gave off some kind of energy that made everybody around me uncomfortable. My gestures were weird. So was my laugh. Sometimes I just didn't seem like a *guy*, more like some kind of alien. I thought back to the 7th grade, when Jenny Chervil and Kendra Harris had said similar things: *Oh good, you're teaching him to be a human.* The fact that Laura sent me a letter every goddamn day wasn't helping matters either. Some of the other boys taunted me about it: *Is that from your girlfriend?* Or rather, I assumed they were taunting me. Since I wasn't used to not being taunted, I didn't know how to take the question at face value. About halfway through my second week, I stopped reading the letters (she kept saying more or less the same thing in them: updates on the weather and how much she missed me) and just opened the envelopes to see if she'd enclosed money.

The day of my flight back to North Carolina, the Pinecrest staff dropped me off at the airport eight hours prior to my departure time, because of course they did. It was a mutual case of good riddance: I didn't have the hunger, my full-body sunburn ached almost as much as my arms and shoulders and legs, and although there'd been no overt bullying this time, it was more of the same shit. I had my own private departure plans. At the airport and alone again, I suppose I said whatever my age-13-almost-14 equivalent of "fuck it" was, checked my suitcase once the counter opened, and found a place to read. I had a couple of books (I think I was rereading *'Salem's Lot*) and enough money for some food and a few games of Q-Bert and Ms. Pac-Man.

At the airport back in Kinston, the Marine didn't recognize me at first, or so Laura told me later. My two weeks in the south Florida sun had scorched me several shades darker. Normally a bleached shade of alabaster with dishwater-blond curls, I'd come home reddish brown, with hair an odd shade of chlorine and platinum.

Later: "I sent you letters every day!" Laura beamed.

Me: "I noticed."

I lasted one more year and quit swimming.

CHAPTER 10: PATTERN RECOGNITION

There have been a few years that changed my life. The tenth grade was one of them. Two major things happened: I got into NCSSM and I learned the truth (albeit with some maternal embroidering) about my paternal grandparents.

The application process for NCSSM was and perhaps still is more complex than college applications. You had to take the Scholastic Aptitude Test, for one thing. Not difficult. There was the initial application form. I loathe filling out forms, always have. Transcripts, if I remember correctly. Then, the agony of waiting to find out if I'd get a campus interview. Atavistically certain I was the kind of kid this school was designed for, I was confident in a terrified way all through the process. When the letter came, advising us that I had been selected for an interview, I was elated but not entirely surprised. The logistics would be a bit of a problem, though: the campus visit would require a trip to Durham the same weekend I also had a swim meet in Greensboro.

Laura took me to JCPenney's to buy nice clothes for the occasion. Having long been the object of middle-school derision for wearing clothes identifiably from Penney's (*"I just love your designer jeans!"* exclaimed one little bitch in my algebra class when she saw the label), I wasn't keen, but beyond grumbling a few protests, there wasn't a lot I could say. There was little point in bringing up the bullies. Apart from literally killing them (I won't say it never crossed my mind), there was nothing left anyone could do about it. Other than leaving. Which was the whole point of buying a suit for the interview. Laura chose a greenish beige blazer and a pair of maroon trousers that I hated on sight. But I had the physique of a stack of driftwood. There wasn't much else that would fit.

"See how the colors match?" She pointed at the tiny, multicolored threads in the weave of the fabric, then at the garish pants. She had a point. There was a certain amount of burgundy in the jacket. Teal, too, and purple, and possibly yellow. But she had the artistic eye in the family, not to mention the checkbook. "They look very handsome together. You look very handsome. And this jacket is *slub silk*! I think it's a real bargain at this price. It's *silk*!"

We had to be on campus at S&M on Saturday, drive another hour and a half west to Greensboro after that, and I think I had a couple of events on that Sunday. No idea how well I did in those, but I liked the school on sight and instantly felt at home there. A former teaching hospital, it had been repurposed as a residential high school. There were already nurses' dormitories on the premises, so only the most basic updates were needed, and the wings of patient rooms also became dorms. Old-growth trees graced the campus, and new landscaping had been put in and cultivated over the four or five years the school had been open—an explosion of springtime flowers everywhere you looked. The whole atmosphere felt lived in but cared for.

As for the students themselves, I'm not sure what I was expecting. Possibly a hive of pallid geeks who talked in mumbles and gave off a low hum when you put a few of them in the same room? A pack of dumpy, multilingual unfuckables who compensated for their fungal complexions by building nuclear warheads in their dorm rooms? The mythology that surrounded the place made the students sound scary. Objectively speaking, I *was* scary, so I figued I'd fit in, but the sheer normalcy of it all was a pleasant surprise.

The interview itself went well—the teacher interviewing me was from Greenville, so perhaps I had a leg up. If I'm honest, I suspect he knew who I was and what I'd been through, and understood that I needed an escape hatch. After the interview, we also had to take a personality test (I think it might have been the Myers-Briggs) and write an essay. Mine was about what would happen if human beings suddenly grew thick fur. I wrote about depilatory creams and flea powder, and how eventually people would stop caring and would start wearing less in public.

The day the acceptance letters were due to arrive, my classmates and I were on edge. Five of us had been shortlisted. One or two had parents at home, called during break, and got the news. Dying of anxiety, I called our next-door neighbor from the guidance counselor's office. Mercifully, the neighbor was home. Waiting for her to walk out to our mailbox and back, I fidgeted. I danced. I was like a little kid who had to pee. An endless few minutes later, she picked up the phone again.

"I think it's good news! It's a really big envelope, not a small one. When you've applied for something, the acceptances usually come in big envelopes and the rejection letters are just one page."

I think I made a keening noise, kind of like a shriek through the nose. I'm pretty sure I also greyed out for a moment or two.

"Want me to open it?" my neighbor asked.

"YES! Please!"

She did.

It was an acceptance.

After thanking her, I ran back to class screaming "I'M GETTING OUT OF HERE! I'M GETTING OUT OF HERE! I'M GETTING OUT OF HERE!" until a teacher stuck her head out of her classroom door and told me to be quiet.

Much of those last few months at Rose High were about saying goodbye to the few friends I had, and about getting ready to go to S&M. There were forms to fill out, classes to register for. Even the bullying let up. Once I was out of E.B. Aycock— then the junior high school—and in the tenth grade at Rose, the worst of it had subsided anyway. The older kids didn't care enough to mess with me (I suspect the older guys on the swim team also had something to do with it) and the dickheads who'd been making my life hell had either flunked out, impregnated sluts, transferred to other schools, or some combination of the above. In any case, I was leaving, nobody was attacking me in the street, and there was the most incredible sense of lightness, of relief.

In retrospect, I can't honestly say that the thermonuclear question I later asked Laura was something I'd been brooding over. If anything, it's got more to do with the way I think. Having always been a writer, assembling stories from the bits and pieces of life, I had an eye for detail and mad pattern-recognition skills. I can put disconnected things together and either find meaning there or create some. It doesn't always take place consciously, either. I notice things, reflect on them, file them away for potential future use. Then, out of the clear blue sky, some realization will strike. Generally, it's an idea for a story, although in this case, it was more about history.

It was inevitable, I suppose, even for someone as programmed not to ask questions as I was, that I'd come to realize the story of my grandmother's death was a lie. There were too many gaping holes to ignore for long, too many blatant inconsistencies. Besides, by the time I was 15, I was mature enough to realize most households weren't as strained and peculiar as ours unless people were keeping awful secrets.

The evidence:

1. The story of the fatal car wreck didn't make an atom of sense. The official version went something like this: *They got in a wreck, and the car caught on fire. Your grandmother burned to death. Your grandfather was thrown out of the car, and he broke his arm.* Several times over the years, and despite the fact that I wasn't supposed to, I had pressed for more details: Did Jewel's head hit the windshield? Was she knocked out? Why couldn't she get out of the car? Why couldn't Patrick help her? Even with a broken arm, wasn't the other arm okay? After all, if your wife's in a burning car and you're not incapacitated, wouldn't you try to pull her out? Was there another car involved? If so, what happened to them? We'd been in a car wreck, a very bad one, and there were other people around to help. Even in the Louisiana countryside, there had to be other people at the scene, so why had no one pulled her from the burning car? Old cars didn't burn so quickly, did they? All that metal? Had it suddenly exploded? The Marine and Laura had been telling the same very basic, very flimsy story for years, answering my questions mostly with exasperated sighs that meant it was time to shut up.

2. Neither the Marine nor Laura had ever explicitly said that my grandfather was dead. I knew my *maternal* grandfather

was dead. Dick died of old age, basically. He had Alzheimer's. (In Granny's Southern Gothic parlance, he went senile.) The Marine's younger sister had died in childhood: spinal meningitis. I knew what those words meant from an early age, and it was yet another of those toxic topics: we weren't supposed to talk about her. Jewel supposedly burning to death in a car accident, though: was it the absence of specific facts that made me suspicious, or was the truth hinted at in the telling? As morbid as Laura could be, with a Southern woman's almost necrophiliac love of family plots, why had there been no in-depth descriptions of his funeral and his burial site? Nor any other details that you would expect, such as how old he'd been when he died, whether the Marine had inherited anything, how he had taken the death?

3. The Marine was estranged from his family. Over the years, there had been hints that he had a whole pack of relatives down near Alexandria, Louisiana, but we'd never met them apart from one visit from his/our Aunt Loretta, who was nice but sort of shrouded in secrecy. How were we related to her, exactly? Why the hushed conversations that we were told not to listen in on? What had happened to cause the estrangement? The answer was always some inchoate, illogical variant on *Very bad things, but don't ask him; he doesn't like to talk about it.*

4. Even without actual secrets to keep, Laura adored drama. *Don't go looking through our locked boxes*, she would say. *There are news articles we don't want you to read yet. There are some things for later, when you're old enough.* If that shit isn't an incentive to hone your lock-picking skills, I don't know what is.

One day, that summer before I went to S&M, I rode to work with Laura. She had come home for lunch. I would spend the afternoon in downtown Greenville: not really shopping, since

I had no money and there wasn't much to buy, but browsing in stores. I'd have a Coke and a pack of nabs from a vending machine, then spend the rest of the afternoon playing video games and reading. She had just parked the car in the big lot behind the student center, where her office was. After she switched the engine off, I hit her with the question that had finally fully resolved itself in my mind: "Dad's mother didn't really die in a car wreck, did she?"

Laura froze. She still had a few minutes to kill before she had to go inside. She hated her boss and tended to put off the start of her working day as long as possible.

"What makes you say that?"

"The story doesn't make sense. You've always said she was killed in a wreck, but, like, there's no detail. Or the details don't add up. And if he was thrown from the car, why did he break his arm? Did he get thrown out an open window, or did he go through the windshield? He should have gotten different injuries." Having been in a couple of car wrecks already, I had a pretty good sense of what could and couldn't happen. And I liked reading the medical encyclopedia we kept at home. "Like head injuries. You've always said they lost control of the car, but did they hit someone else? Who did they hit, or who hit them? If they went into the ditch, what happened to make the car catch fire?"

Laura looked decidedly uncomfortable, said she had to go inside, but later, she'd tell me the rest.

It was worse than anything I had imagined.

Patrick was a dreamer, she said that evening. Always looking for a way to get rich quick. They lived in a converted chicken coop for a while, and had upgraded to a camper. Jewel had been a raging bitch, too: she made him miserable, and, well, he took out a life insurance policy on her. He convinced a cousin to do the same with his own wife, too. They hired two men from the factory where he worked. The idea was to rape the two wives and then beat them to death. At the last minute, though, the cousin lost his nerve and backed out of the deal. Patrick chose to proceed by himself. How he delivered his wife to her murderers, Laura didn't say. She just prayed Jewel had died early in the act, to lessen her suffering. There couldn't be many worse fates than living long enough to burn to death in a car after being raped and beaten almost to death, unless perhaps you also knew your husband was behind it.

"Did she know?" I asked. "Or could she have known?"

Laura wasn't sure.

Intending to hide the evidence, Patrick and his accomplices staged a car wreck: they put Jewel's (presumably dead) body in the car and set it on fire. First, for added verisimilitude, one of them also drove over Patrick's forearm, crushing it under the tire. With this injury, he would then claim to have been thrown from the car and knocked out.

For a time, the Louisiana cops believed the story, but Patrick's sudden lavish spending attracted attention. Laura said he had a mistress somewhere (which probably means I have bastard cousins out there somewhere, but I've also long been reconciled to the idea that I might have a Vietnamese half-sibling or two I'll never meet as well), and the woman began wearing a new fur coat. He bought one for Laura, as well, and shipped it to her. I seem to remember her telling me he bought a Cadillac, too. The local sheriff got suspicious, made some phone calls, and discovered the insurance policy. After that, things happened fast: Patrick and his two accomplices went to prison. In fact, Laura said the judge was so disgusted by the whole thing that he pledged Patrick would never be released. Not while he, the judge, was alive, anyway. However, he predeceased Patrick, and the next judge to take the bench granted parole, much to the dismay of the Marine's family.

It didn't take him long to get involved in another murder: this time, he drove the getaway car when a couple of other men held up a convenience store. They shot and killed the clerk behind the counter. They got caught. Patrick went back to prison, a life sentence this time.

"He's still *there*?" I asked.

Laura nodded.

"We couldn't tell you all these years because you just weren't old enough to understand."

For once, I agreed with her.

"*Do not*, under any circumstances, tell your sister this. I don't think she's ready to hear it yet."

For once, I agreed with that too. A grandfather who had done these terrible things wasn't someone I wanted to talk about, much less meet. I'd already had as much "together as a family" as I could take; the idea of having more damaged relatives whose troubles I'd have to absorb made me want to run the other way even faster. I'd be leaving for Durham in a couple of months, and there didn't seem to be anything I could do with this knowledge. As much as I could, I pushed this story out of my head and focused on my escape plans.

PART TWO: S&M

CHAPTER 11: A BIG BOX WITH ALL OUR LIVES IN IT

The left front wheel of our shopping cart wobbled and squeaked, ratcheting up the tension as the Marine and Laura loaded it up with items they thought I'd need at school. We had been in Kmart half an hour already, much longer than we usually spent. Impulsively they pulled things off the shelves and tossed them in: a couple of packages of Bic Crystal pens, a few packages of notebook paper, a packet of markers. If I had suggested coloring books and finger paints, they'd have said yes. Laura's hands were shaking.

Did I want folding, portable bookshelves? Well, I had plenty of books; why not? Make that two! Christmas in August. In the first draft of this memoir, I wrote "The Marine was in one of his rare generous moods," but that doesn't even come close. I had never seen him like this before. If he was buying, I was saying yes. A director's chair? Yes, of course. Laura compared the ones with blue canvas seats against the yellow ones. She liked yellow better. It reminded her of her car, a yellow Datsun B210 station wagon. "We should get the yellow one. It's such a sunny color—a *happy* color," she said, making two sentences out of half a thought. She beamed at me, her face unusually taut.

Paul, my roommate-as-of-the-next day, had called to say his

father bought a dorm-sized refrigerator, so we wouldn't need to pick up one of those. A fluorescent desk lamp and a new alarm clock landed in the cart. Squeak squeak squeak, went the wobbly shopping cart, increasingly overburdened.

The Marine ran a finger through his thinning brown hair and farted. Being mostly deaf in one ear, he couldn't hear himself, but Laura blushed, put a hand over her mouth, turned to me, and giggled. As the Marine wandered ahead, either to get a closer look at staplers or to move into unscented air, Laura made an exaggerated face and fanned herself. She rolled her eyes and clamped her hands around her throat.

"Grody to the max!" she exclaimed, still giggling. A fat lady down the aisle heard her and turned to look, her own face puffy and annoyed. "Isn't that right? That's just... *grody!*"

The Marine turned to look back at us, noticed Laura's histrionics, pursed his lips, and glared at her. He didn't say anything. Laura's laughter decomposed into a pout right away. She fumbled in her purse for a second, produced a roll of Rolaids, and handed them over. He accepted an antacid tablet and chewed it, still glaring at her. I noticed grey strands in his eyebrows. I probably wasn't supposed to know about the Grecian Formula under his sink. For that matter, I probably also wasn't supposed to know about the box of Trojans at the bottom of the drawer in his nightstand. I guessed I could understand the Grecian Formula, but not the Trojans. Laura had had a hysterectomy. She didn't have any insides left to get pregnant with. I looked away. Only a few hours left and I'd be in Durham, a hundred miles west of Greenville, for the next nine months. Still a bit too close for my liking (I now live on the other goddamn side of the planet and it's still a bit too close for my liking), but it would do. It was a start.

And where was Janelle? Somewhere in the store, probably trying to decide which heavy-metal album to buy. Looking back, I don't think she ever truly liked mid-'80s hair metal; she listened to it to make a statement and irk the rest of us. In Janelle's world, people were divided into two opposing camps: preps and punks. A real punk from Thatcher's grotty England would have cut someone's face for conflating them with Twisted Sister, but Janelle didn't seem to know that. I once asked her which one I was. Her answer sort of surprised me and sort of didn't: I wanted to be a prep but I wasn't very convincing and the other preps didn't like me, but neither did the punks. Nothing new there. She didn't want anything to do with us, anyway, especially since I was leaving for S&M in the morning. Not to put too fine a point on it, I was getting out and she wasn't.

My relationship with her has always been complicated. As kids, I was always told how much I was supposed to love my little sister. But then, Laura was always telling us what our feelings were supposed to be instead of asking us what they were. "Look at that big smile! You're so happy now!" or "You're just sad because you didn't cut a full second off your 50 free. You'll feel better tomorrow," or "You're not really *like that*, even if the other kids say it all the time." It's not empathy when the other person fundamentally doesn't get that you exist as a separate human being and not an extension of themselves, a baby spider plant on the end of a stalk. Because of my achievements and Janelle's disability, I got one kind of attention and she got the other. She resented me for being a boy, for getting good grades, for being a good swimmer. Now and then, she'd flare up and remind me that her IQ was as high as mine but that she had the potential to do even better: "I'm younger, so I can learn from your mistakes!" I never wanted there to be a competition in the first place, and I had more than enough on my hands dealing with the constant bullying and my horrible, growing awareness that the bullies were actually right—I *was* a fag—to contend with Janelle's seething cauldron of resentment, envy, and contempt.

She looked up to me and looked down on me at the same time. I was an over-achieving swimmer who got straight As in school, and was a boy, so on paper I should have ticked all the boxes. I was also an awkward dork, and the designated school fag, and while it would be going too far to say I had no friends, I kind of didn't. In the four years I spent in the Greenville public school system, I can count the number of times I was invited to a party or something on the fingers of one hand. Ergo, I played with Janelle. We built a city for her dolls (she had some Barbies and those Strawberry Shortcake dolls that smelled like the car deodorizers you hang on your rearview mirror) in the upstairs playroom. The Marine hated that I played with them but when you don't have friends and your eyes are tired from reading, you take what you can get. One time when we took them outside, he lost his shit, started shouting at me, picked me up, carried me down to the edge of the pond, and threw me in.

"You've ruined him! You've ruined him!" he screamed at Laura. *"Look at what you've done to him!"*

After that, I did my best to avoid being alone with him. Now, in the supermarket, we were down to a matter of hours.

"Why don't I just go and see where Janelle got herself off to?" Laura said, looking deep into her purse, as if she had to be careful to put the Rolaids back exactly where she had found them.

"Good idea," the Marine said.

As Laura waddled off, he looked at me for a long moment, long enough to make me fidget. I hadn't really said anything and didn't intend to.

"Sometimes your mother's sense of humor is a little bit strange," he said. I didn't know how to read the look on his face and took half a step back. He'd once belted me for falling out of the treehouse he'd built in the back yard and knocking the wind out of myself. Although I didn't think he was going to hit me in the grocery store (that had stopped a few years before, after I hit him back after a belting—or possibly it was when another swim-team parent noticed the stripes on the backs of my legs), he wasn't predictable. He withdrew his wallet from a back pocket, opened it, and gave me two $20 bills. "Don't tell her about this," he said.

I suspected I was being bribed but I couldn't tell for what.

"Okay."

After Kmart, we stopped off at Kroger's for groceries. It was just as weird as the Kmart trip had been. In the candy aisle, another mood swing took him and he barked "You'd better be brushing your teeth up there... and you'd better be eating enough roughage. If I hear you're getting cavities—or getting constipated—I'll jerk you out of there so fast you won't know what happened to you."

That night, I had to finish packing. Although you would think I'd have done it weeks earlier, my lack of punctuality was already entrenched by then. In the eighth grade, I started to admire the kids who rushed into class the second the bell rang, and cultivated a habit of making what I saw as (or hoped were) glamorously frazzled entrances after that. It didn't make me cool and convey a social life like the kids I admired had, but I imagined I was getting something socially useful out of the practice of dashing into the classroom, books already spilling out of my hands, and flinging myself into my seat, a split-second before the teacher could legitimately mark me down as tardy. Accessible rebellion, perhaps. Troublemaker training wheels.

I took the same approach to packing. The idea wasn't to cause stress and discord in my family by having shoved only half of what I meant to take to Durham with me into boxes by 9.00pm the night before leaving. I didn't care what they thought as I sat in my room picking out which books to take (the Stephen King and Peter Straub ones) and which ones to leave until later. This required me to re-read all their dust-jacket synopses, even though I'd read each book two or three times already. I'd have to take pretty much all my clothes, because there was no telling how soon I'd go home again, and the more shit I had to wear, the less often I'd have to do laundry. Laura was downstairs cooking her specialty spaghetti and meatballs. The sauce was yummy because she flavored it with generous amounts of Taylor Lake Country Red wine. She would pour in a big dollop, then drink a glass of Taylor Lake Country White while she stirred the sauce. Then she'd pour in another dollop, then drink another glass. If she was feeling frisky, then she'd drink a glass of Taylor Lake Country Pink. The meatballs and my mother would keep simmering in their respective sauces for another hour or so until dinner was ready. We were eating really late tonight, but it was a weird night. I put on my then-favorite Eurythmics album, the *1984* soundtrack, and turned up the volume to drown out the screechy crap Janelle was listening to.

Greenville was a small town then. Not so much anymore, but back then the population was only about 35,000, plus another 15,000 or so ECU students. When I made my rounds of the liquor and grocery stores, collecting cardboard boxes, almost everybody knew what I was up to. Cashiers and other shoppers would ask my mother, "You gettin' ready to take your boy up to that school in Durham, ittn't that right? The one for the smart ones? You mus' be real proud." I'd smile at them, blushing scarlet, and walk out to Laura's yellow station wagon with another stack of Crown Royal or Seagrams 7 boxes, hoping my ass didn't swish like the Marine kept insisting it did. I knew that everywhere I went, my every move was scrutinized. I no longer believed Laura's stories of telepathic monitoring. It was just the reality of being a small-town homo who hadn't actually come out to himself yet.

"You don' look like you're ready to see 'im go, but I can tell he's gettin' pretty anxious." I tried not to stick around for these conversations, because Laura's face would squinch up like she had a migraine coming on. She'd cast despairing Bassett Hound eyes at me, then put on a broadly false smile and recite one of her lines about what a great opportunity I'd been given, how the Ivy League schools would be fighting over me, that kind of thing.

"Do you have any more boxes?" was all I'd ask.

"Just go look back in the storage room, by the refrigerators."

"Thank you, ma'am."

Since Laura's Datsun wasn't big enough to hold the four of us plus all my shit, we borrowed Granny's Mercury station wagon for the day.

I drove. Already completely unhinged, Laura gibbered objections: I didn't have enough experience driving a fully loaded car to make the trip safely. The Marine shut her up by insisting the best way to get that experience was by just doing it. I broke the tie by announcing I'd pull over if I couldn't handle it, and I'd let them navigate through Durham when we got there.

By the start of the school year, the worst of the summer weather was past us. Still, it was shaping up to be a warm day: even at 8.00 in the morning, the layers of heat were already piling up. I turned the air conditioner up to full blast, to turn the interior of the car into the Arctic as soon as possible and perhaps to stop the nervous sweat that was already rolling down my torso from my armpits. Granny's car had light floaty power steering, which meant the slightest twitch of the steering wheel sent the car skittering in a different direction. The Marine sat in the passenger seat looking whitewashed and grim. Laura, choked up, took a seat in the back, next to my sister, who had on her Walkman and was ignoring the rest of us.

I wanted to be driving a Ferrari, not a big whale of a station wagon with my fretting parents. Anything to get me out of there faster. When I started accelerating above 60, The Marine would bark, "Slow it down!"

About the fourth time this happened, on Highway 264 near Wilson, he switched to "Slow it down, got-dammit!"

"Just remember, son, this is just a big box with all our lives in it," Laura offered.

I flinched, and the car swerved dramatically.

"Jesus Christ, Laura!" my father said.

Janelle started bumping, her damaged-childhood habit that had never gone away. *Bonk, bonk, bonk.* I could feel the wheel twitch every time she collided with the seatback behind me.

"Well, it's true!" Laura protested. "Our lives are all in his hands right now. It's important that he knows he needs to drive responsibly. I'm just trying to emphasize that with him. That's not unreasonable is it, son?"

Bump, bump, bump. The car rocked. I didn't say anything.

Somehow I got us there.

My first night at NCSSM was like going to a big sleepover with new friends, albeit without games of Truth or Dare and potential embarrassing parental interruptions just when someone's pants had come off. The Marine and Laura couldn't leave soon enough for my liking. I'd maxed out on Laura's overly touchy, clutching anguish and the Marine's wild fluctuation between Mr. Reasonable and his erratic anger-golem persona.

Most of the boys on my hall had arrived with a few suitcases, nothing more, like guests checking into their hotel rooms. By comparison, I was moving in. The Mercury wagon sat low on its suspension because I'd loaded it up. Books, chairs, the frames for the loft beds, posters, random personal items... people noticed, and gravitated toward Paul's and my room. Years later, I was talking to somebody who remembered my arrival at NCSSM. Whoever it was said that each year there were one or two students who were clearly *moving out*. They would bring their shit from home, send their parents off with the requisite goodbyes, and heave a big sigh of relief to be done with them. That was me, this person said.

As we unpacked, there were a few grumbles: "Do you have every book Stephen King has ever published?" (The answer: "No, because there's a limited-edition one called *The Dark Tower*, and I haven't been able to find it.") The lofts went up in about 20 minutes each, and we commenced to set up our desks—massive old wooden things from the '50s, left over from NCSSM's prior incarnation as a teaching hospital—underneath them. Paul brought a rug and a gigantic stereo system. When we were done, it was the only room that looked as if somebody *lived* there. Every other room on the hall had a just-passing-through look: a couple of suitcases, a clock radio, a bed with prison-like ticking covering the mattress, one or two posters taped to the walls. We didn't exactly become the Cool New Guys on the Hall but we had more stuff, and from that first day, ours was the room where people hung out.

CHAPTER 12: WHERE A+ STUDENTS GET CS

At one of the information sessions for the new class of juniors, a speaker had cautioned the audience: "NCSSM is where A+ students get Cs. If you want to do well here, you have to *work*. Plan on spending at least four hours a night on homework. *At least.*" Having never in my life spent more than four hours a *week* on homework, even in the advanced classes at Rose High, I didn't believe it. At Rose, I'd developed a strategy: I would sit in the back of the room in afternoon classes, listening with one ear while getting work from *other* classes done, prioritizing the subjects with the heaviest textbooks in order to keep from lugging them home. It's harder to outrun bullies when you're loaded down with books. This way, I could usually finish most or all of my homework before leaving school for the day. Classwork took little time and less effort, and I never did reading assignments because the teachers talked about everything in class and I could retain it.

When I got home from school most days, I was done. I'd read or watch reruns of *Star Trek* and *Bewitched*, or depending on the time of year, spend some time in the garden. I liked growing herbs and had built raised beds after reading about them in one of the Marine and Laura's survivalist books. A nursery over in

Plymouth, about an hour away, specialized in herbs, and Granny would drive me now and then. In addition to kitchen basics like mint, oregano, basil, and about five different kinds of thyme, I grew exotics: wormwood, celandine, santolina. Apart from the wormwood, these would usually die. The lavender baked in the Southern heat, and the rosemary tended to give up on life after a couple of months, turning brown and dropping needles like a Christmas tree on a January curbside. I tried anyway. I could putter around out there for an hour or so, pulling weeds and gazing at the sinkhole that had opened up in the ground just on the other side of the fence separating our property from the golf course. Why didn't someone from the country club come along to fill it up? What would it be like to climb down inside? Would the ground clamp shut around me like a giant mouth, like in that horrifying scene in Peter Straub's novel *Floating Dragon*? Then, in the evening, there would be swim practice. Two hours of sprints and laps. Bromine sting in my eyes and my sinuses. As time wore on and I got tired, I would hear my gargling grunts as I pulled myself through water that seemed to grow denser and denser. This is how I spent my afternoons and evenings, not doing homework. How much harder could S&M possibly be?

At S&M, many teachers assign a ton of reading in order to establish basic concepts in advance, reserving classroom time to focus on application and exploration. Regardless of the subject, gone was the compensation for the dunces and dull normals who hadn't mastered the basics. For the first time in our lives, we were being taught at a suitable level. I found this part refreshing, but the school didn't offer much to transition us out of a lifetime of not having to try. Though we had the intellectual capacity, the maturity was a separate issue, and the school just threw us into the deep end, so to speak. The mythology preceding our arrival NCSSM had been that the courses were *hard*. As it turned out, they actually weren't. Not really. There was no concept thrown at us that we weren't well enough equipped between the ears to understand and apply. What it boiled down to was, as the Marine would have put it, buckling down and doing the work.

To be honest, that wasn't what I was there for, even if I'd have denied it at the time. The exultation in having escaped Greenville and my family eclipsed the grinding realities of NCSSM. I was more excited to have friends, to be able to walk down the hall without somebody calling me a faggot, and to get back to my room at the end of the day without having to face parental derangement than I was to be taking courses in organic chemistry and electronic music. (I signed up for the music course naively thinking I would come out of it making synth-pop like Eurythmics or Depeche Mode, and was only too happy to split the cost of a reverb with Mark Morrow. Our magnum opus was a boring, atonal, and unlistenable excrescence of spoken-word mutterings littered with synthesizer squonks here and there. I think it had something to do with cows.)

When I got there in the fall of '85, the school had only been open about five years. Different amenities had opened at different times. The cafeteria, for example. The senior boys on my hall (second Wyche) told horror stories of having to walk four blocks down 9th Street to eat at the canteen in a neighboring elementary school, E.K. Powe. By all accounts, the food was terrible, earning the place the nickname Icky Poo. Although S&M's cafeteria had been open a year or so by the time I arrived, the New Dorm (known as Nude while it was under construction and for at least a year after it opened; now named Hunt) wasn't ready yet, meaning some of the boys had to be housed at the Carolina Duke Motor Inn half a mile away and bussed to and from campus throughout the day. Being assigned to Wyche left me with mixed feelings: it was a lot more convenient to live on campus (I could go back to the dorm to use the bathroom if I had to), but Wyche was—to put it kindly—kind of a dump. According to a joke I heard later, it would be the safest place on campus if the Russians bombed us. We could shelter in the basement and the cockroaches in the walls would absorb the radiation.

As you'd expect, my first friendships were with guys on my hall. Paul (who bore more than a passing resemblance to the lead singer of the Norwegian band A-ha and accentuated the similarities with the leather bands around one wrist, long bangs, and a carefully cultivated aura of being the coolest guy in the room) and I hit it off: both into music, we had hundreds of albums and 12" remix singles. And it was the '80s, not exactly history's worst decade for music (that would be the '90s). There was a loose group of about seven of us: Mark Morrow, Martin Finch, Cyrus Erickson, Alex McLawhorn, and Rich Anderson. Geeks all, we bonded over frozen pizza, teen angst, and Pink Floyd on Thursday nights. Now and then, others would drift through. Palmer McCall, who lived downstairs, was from a small town in the mountains. Smart and detached and a bit daffy all at the same time, he generally *was* the coolest guy in the room. His first car was a hearse (he and his sisters had named it Patty Hearse). One of his sisters lived in England and he had spent time there, hence his collection of Smiths records and his fondness for using Elmer's School Glue in lieu of styling gel. Rich's roommate Sam Gondry (whom I suspected was gay too) would wander by now and then, but he brought an air of regal condescension with him. The rest of us were too young to recognize it as a mask for insecurity. Sam liked snacking on crackers and Roquefort. Rich nicknamed the stuff "shit cheese" and would often take refuge in our room until the stink subsided and he could go to sleep without gagging.

Two weeks after the school year began, I went back to Greenville for my first weekend home, more because I thought it was expected than because I actually wanted to. Mostly I wanted to eat better food. It's not that Laura had spectacular skills in the kitchen, but even her "throw it all out" dinners (in which she served warmed-up leftovers plus goodies like Vienna sausages and canned pineapple chunks speared with tasseled toothpicks as a festive touch) appealed to me more than the institutional dreck we were being fed. In the cafeteria's defense, the milk was usually not rancid and we could usually identify what we were eating without needing to examine it under a microscope borrowed from one of the labs upstairs. At home, I did laundry and cringed when Laura came into my bedroom to tuck me in. I didn't miss the mortifying zit-popping ritual. If I could keep her from touching me more than the bare minimum without causing a spasm of pouting, I would call it a win.

It turned out I wasn't the only one feeling a rush of "oh thank God" when I got back to campus: quite a lot of us felt that way after home visits. But my reprieve from parental mortification didn't last long: the Marine, Laura, and Janelle came up for a visit a couple of weeks later, the better to subject Paul and me to an afternoon *en famille*. It went well enough: lunch somewhere, a bit of shopping, maybe an early dinner, no more than the level of family awkwardness anyone would have expected. I made the mistake of thinking the day would pass without any bizarro bombshells being dropped. Then, leaving, Laura was commenting on our record collections. Paul had even more vinyl than I did. He was a bit dubious of some of my choices (he didn't like Prince and Depeche Mode), but no matter: I was pleased with my newest purchase, a comeback album from one of the legends of Motown. Laura, apparently thinking she'd score a few cool points with the young'uns, made a racist joke based on a certain assonant similarity between the R&B artist's first name and an undignified body part. If ever there had been a moment for the mists to roll in and erase a moment, this would have been it. Paul looked at me in horror. Laura continued her leer, looking back and forth between the two of us, mouth slightly open, lower lip moving goldfish-like in anticipation of either the laughs she expected us to burst into or the pout she would need in case her joke failed.

"Oh my God," I said. It was all I could manage. "Oh my God. Oh my God."

Janelle was lost in the squall of her Walkman, but to the Marine's credit, a flash of disgust roiled his face before he could get it under control.

"Jesus Christ, Laura. We need to get on home."

Later, Paul said, "I think I understand why you're here."

There wasn't much more either of us could say. I met his own family several times: his parents were pleasant enough, nice without being smarmy or patronizing, and they seemed to understand concepts like boundaries and age-appropriate behavior. His father didn't have a face like a storm cloud and his mother didn't look like an escapee from the borderlands between screams and sedation. Paul's brother Stewart was friendly and would sometimes hang out with us when we went to see movies off campus.

These glimpses of relative normality seemed to confirm something I'd already noticed back in Greenville: my parents weren't *like* other people. One thing the Marine and Laura shared was a seething resentment of their mutual lot in life. The Marine would trudge in at the end of the day and groan, "Son, when you get older, find a way to work for yourself. Find a way to make your own money." He would then disappear into a bottle. Laura's own rage took a different form when it boiled over: the fact that she'd been denied a college education meant she'd been relegated to a lifetime of work far beneath her potential. In the rural South, there weren't many opportunities for a woman to be the smartest guy in the room. Hence, a smiley version of passive-aggression became her weapon of choice. Then there was the question of religion, which the Marine and Laura only paid lip service to. After they got married, the Marine left his both his family and their creepy Pentecostal Holiness background in Louisiana and started attending Episcopalian services with Laura. They went to church because it was expected, never mind that they didn't believe a word of it. It was what people *did*. They went through the motions for some years after Janelle and I were born, then just quit, preferring to spend those hours on Sunday-afternoon drives instead of on hard wooden pews yawning through drivel from the Bible.

As the weeks turned into months at S&M and I looked back from a distance, I could see that for all their nuttiness, there were occasional things they'd done right. Noting how obsessed all the students were with their SAT scores, I began to think that the Marine and Laura's refusal to tell me my IQ score had not been such a bad idea. I appreciated the freedom from religion, too, as I was beginning to notice that the devout seemed to have flypaper wrapped around their minds to keep ideas from getting in. I could also see faint signs that the Marine had changed. There had been a thaw, albeit a subtle one: less prone to ranting and craziness (I didn't realize yet that I was seeing less of him and he was hiding it), now he was simply checked out. To compensate for this new and occasionally almost engaging emotional absence (not that there had ever been an emotional presence) Laura panicked and clung... to me, mainly, because it was also more and more obvious that he couldn't stand her. Janelle couldn't either.

Desperate to put them and Greenville and basically every other aspect of my life behind me, I wasted no time in trying to revamp my image a bit. Having always hated my curly hair, I decided to put it to better use: I grew it out and bleached the top like the guys in Depeche Mode. At Northgate Mall, I found an accessory shop willing to pierce my ear without checking my ID (I just told the girl I was 16 and she got out the hole-puncher). It felt like a cross between a jab and an electric shock, faded to a slow-burn sting, and later lingered as a warmly distracting ache. As far as my clothes were concerned, the kindest thing I can say is that I looked like a crayon factory blew up and I was standing too close. I had an excuse, though. It was the '80s. Think Culture Club, Duran Duran, early-career Madonna. Loud colors, big padded shoulders, and hair boofed up like you were standing with one hand on a Van de Graaff generator. Lavender paisley shirt, burgundy shorts, and green socks? Sure, why not? At S&M, I could treat myself like a blank canvas, so to speak, but the boy once deemed to need lessons in how to be a human was still there no matter how much I tried to paint over him.

At times, the urge to tell Paul, Alex, and a couple of the other guys I was getting closer to about my grandfather was overwhelming. What always stopped me was the look of genuine fear on Laura's face when she told me the story. There was always drama with her but this was different. I didn't want one more reason for people to consider me a pariah. It had never occurred to me that she wasn't worried so much about the story getting out as about *him* getting out, that we had all those guns in the house for a reason. So I went about my studies in a distracted way, at first doing the minimum I thought I could get away with and getting Bs and Cs for my efforts. Shocked by my first report card (a B in PE?—how was that even *possible*?), I began doing the work. For the first time in my life, I was studying, and my grades after that first few months rose accordingly. (Also common, remarked a couple of teachers.) Although I didn't love having so much of my free time eaten up by schoolwork, well, I'd signed up for this. Besides, we were all in it together. I could do this, I told myself. I had what it took. More than. I could do this.

CHAPTER 13: FORT WORTH

There were only two phones on each hall in Wyche. They were the old-fashioned black rotary ones, and best not to look too closely at the generations of earwax calcifying in the tiny holes of each earpiece. Each phone booth was a wooden closet with a single grimy window made of wire-mesh safety glass. The paint on the bench and the varnish on the door had been reapplied year after year, producing an almost-lovely institutional nacre that begged to have graffiti carved into it with a key or the nib of a dead ballpoint pen. Everyone on the hall shared these phones; no one had a private line (during my senior year, one of the guys on my hall tapped into an existing line and set one up in his room), and the first cell phones had only gone on the market some two years before. Very few people had them. I generally got calls from my parents every few days. Laura would call and go on about how much she missed me. (She also sent cloying letters almost daily at first, telling me the same thing. By the end of my first semester there, I had mostly stopped reading them, just as I'd done at Pinecrest two summers prior.) She'd talk in ominously vague but laden terms about how things at home weren't going well. She wouldn't come right out and say it, but I had a feeling divorce was in the air. This didn't surprise me: after all, since about the age of four, I had suspected my parents would get divorced. Although they claimed to love each other very much, I got no sense whatsoever of them *liking* each other.

On the phone, these rants of hers peeled back the years: I was a little kid in the passenger seat of her station wagon again, riding home at the end of the day, and she was going on and on about what a bastard her boss was. I don't think the term *micromanaging* had been invented yet but that's what he was doing, and it was driving her crazy. *Everything* was driving her crazy. Oh, and would it be okay if we don't send you your allowance this week because there's no money for groceries? (In person, she tended to slip these requests in just as we were getting home to our immense house in upscale Brook Valley.) I learned to hold the phone a few inches away from my ear while Laura droned on: how Granny was "going behind" (Laura said this for years and by the time Granny finally went, back in 2006, I'm amazed there was actually anything left of her), how the Marine seemed more and more withdrawn, how Janelle just listened to loud music and bumped for hours at a time, the usual unusual. I'd hold the phone far enough away to follow the rhythmic buzz but not hear the words. After a suitable length of time, I'd put it back to my ear and find a place to insert a grunt or some other interjection to make it sound as if I'd been listening. Eventually I stopped feeling bad about doing this. She needed a receptacle, not a listener, and at least this was better than being trapped in the car while she was ranting. Then she'd put the Marine on, and he'd bark gruff advice: find a girlfriend, focus on my studies, find a girlfriend, go out for sports, find a girlfriend. Now and then he'd send me a little extra money (*Don't tell your mother*) for me to use on dates. I spent this money on records because no one wanted to go out with me except for one gay guy, a senior, who sent me into a panic spiral by asking me out when I was still deep in denial.

I'd been at S&M barely two months when the call came. It was the Marine this time. Patrick had died, he said, in the state prison in Louisiana. He confessed that at first he'd been angry with Laura for telling me (*But I figured it out for myself!*, I protested, and he said she'd told him the same thing), but now he was relieved not to have to break the news to both Janelle and me. How did I feel about it?

I didn't, honestly. My feelings, to the extent that I could sort out what they were, still centered around dumbstruck relief at being in a less toxic environment where nobody called me a faggot and I didn't have to dumb myself down. So the skeleton in the family closet could finally stop rattling and lie still in its grave? Terrific. I'd never met my grandfather, nor even known he was even alive until a few months before. It meant nothing and it changed everything. In the moment, there was simply nothing to feel, nothing to give name to.

Laura's account of the story was more sobering, when he put her on the line: Janelle had been in the living room when the call came.

The Marine answered the phone, heard the news, and stammered, "*What?* My father's dead?"

Janelle, hearing this, started screaming: "MY GRANDFATHER WAS ALIVE? MY GRANDFATHER HAS BEEN ALIVE ALL THIS TIME? WHY DIDN'T YOU TELL ME? HOW *COULD* YOU?" In hysterics, she ran upstairs to her room, locked the door (something the Marine used to belt us for doing—he went apeshit if we so much as shut our bedroom doors while he was at home), and started bumping.

They tried to explain it to her, but she was inconsolable; worse, upon learning I already knew, she started screaming again. Never mind that I'd figured it out for myself. She was furious with them, furious with me, furious with the world.

"But remember, you can't tell *anyone!*" Laura reminded me before hanging up. "Think of what people would say, if they knew!"

Back in my room afterward, all I could do was mumble some incoherent bullshit about my grandfather dying. We weren't close, I barely knew him, he and my father were estranged, and I wasn't going to the funeral. There were awkward, desultory condolences. We then went back to doing our homework and I went to class the next day as if nothing had happened. I probably didn't even mention it to my teachers.

The Marine flew down to Louisiana by himself for the funeral, which was taking place over the Thanksgiving holiday. Apart from the visit from Aunt Loretta, it would be his first time seeing his family in—well, in my lifetime, at least. For Thanksgiving, Laura, Janelle, and I flew down to Texas to visit Ray and Nancy Towers. Nancy and Laura had been friends since high school but had fallen out of touch after they'd both gotten married. I think they'd been close when Laura and Joe, her previous fiancé, were together. I inferred that her dumping him for the Marine had caused a rupture, but this was on the Things We're Never Going to Talk About list. So we flew down to DFW, where Ray and Nancy met us at the airport and drove us back to their home in Fort Worth, smoking one cigarette after another in the car. By the time we got to their house, Janelle and I reeked and could barely breathe; we had to open the windows in spite of the cold snap that had hit North Texas.

The whole time we were there, we didn't see much. There was a quick, obligatory drive through downtown Fort Worth. We dutifully looked up at the tall buildings that looked more or less like the ones in Richmond and Greensboro. (Raleigh and Durham didn't have skylines to speak of in the mid-'80s. Because of the high water table and sandy soil, Greenville has a height restriction, which means most buildings top out at four stories.) Dinner at a steakhouse in a large shopping mall. Subfreezing weather, shocking given how far south we were. The two things I remember from that trip are trying brisket for the first time and liking it very much (I no longer eat beef, though), and finding the UK 12" singles from the first Tears for Fears album *The Hurting* and buying them. It was too cold to spend time outdoors, and we mainly seemed to be there so that Laura could spend time with Nancy. There were hushed, late-night talks. Ice clinked in glasses. A couple more ashtray-scented but otherwise forgettable days passed, and then it was time to fly back to North Carolina. Laura was weepy in the airport, weepy on the plane, yet weirdly adamant that we not take pictures of the airline food. She had a couple of drinks on the flight and fell asleep, much to my relief.

After that trip, the phone calls from home darkened with each passing week, weather reports in advance of a hurricane churning toward the Gulf Coast after trashing the Caribbean. Laura would tell me how well she and the Marine were getting along: "Oh," she'd sigh. "I just don't know. I guess things are a little better this week. I just think something must have happened down there in Louisiana when he went to the funeral." There was a certain amount of violence in the background, as well. Nothing particularly new there, only that Janelle's already-mediocre grades had plunged and he was beating the crap out of her when she flunked tests and got Ds on her report cards. Laura wouldn't say so in so many words, but her compulsion to spin a dramatic yarn overshadowed her powers of discretion.

She dropped hints like depth charges.

One night, the Marine lost his mind completely. I no longer remember what set him off, if I ever knew in the first place: Janelle got an F on a major test, or perhaps she'd been caught smoking again. He may also have had a bad day at work, followed by more of Laura's nutty/needy passive aggression, more than his usual few drinks, or some combination of the above. He threw Janelle to the floor in the kitchen and was waling on her, first with his hand and then with his belt when he could unbuckle it and drag it from around his waist (or so Laura told me on the phone right after it happened), bellowing at her the whole time. When Laura stepped in to intervene, he raised his hand as if to hit her too. Janelle stood up and got in between them: "You can punish me, but you will *not* hit my mother."

This calmed him down, at least until the red vapors took him again: he ordered her to bring him a pair of scissors from the kitchen and kneel next to his armchair. He then reached around and cut the rat-tail plait (it was the '80s, remember) off the back of her hair, handed it back to her, and told her to go write him what Laura described it as a prayer. Janelle was supposed to apologize for her behavior, acknowledge his sacrifices for the family, and promise to bring up her grades. She then had to take this back to him and read it while kneeling next to his chair, after which she was to go back to her room, grounded for the next couple of weeks.

This left me far more unsettled than any of the previous calls had, including the news that Patrick was dead. Growing up, I had always borne the brunt of the beatings, and for the first time, it occurred to me that they might not have stopped when I left. With the disappointingly awkward and faggy oldest son around to serve as a punching bag, Janelle was more or less sheltered. Because of her gender and her disability, expectations were lower; I was the boy the Marine got, not the one he wanted; therefore, I required beating like a sword in a forge. I didn't want to ask what was really going on, what they weren't telling me. Was he hitting Janelle? He had to be. But Laura? He'd never hit her before, that I knew of, apart from the spanking that she bragged about, the one the night they met. For the first time, I wondered whether that was actually the truth. After all, the narrative of our whole fucking lives was knit up of secrets and lies under a dime-store Halloween mask of normalcy. What else weren't they telling us?

I couldn't focus on my studies. Latin was easy, so I was still doing well in that class. I won second or third in a statewide competition without even realizing I'd entered it. Sometime during that blur, I began hearing I was one of the Latin gods on campus. That was the S&M nickname for someone known to excel in a certain subject—or, given the context, not just to excel but to be scary good. Such-and-such was a math god, or a calculus god, or a physics god, or what have you. I achieved godhood. It meant nothing and I barely noticed. Math, whatever science classes I was taking, electronic music, the art class… it was a blur. I kept trying to focus and kept failing because no matter how far away I now was, I still couldn't get away from my family. I didn't want anything bad to happen to them, but for the first time, I was beginning to see that the two hours between Durham and Greenville was still not enough distance.

I couldn't eat, either. At the time, NCSSM had a work-service program: three hours a week helping out around campus. As with most such things, the idea was good but the implementation fell short. As juniors, we had to do one semester in either the cafeteria or on the grounds crew. The next semester, we'd be assigned to a teacher or someone in the administration. Somehow, despite my love of gardening, I was assigned to the cafeteria in my first semester. It was as vile as it sounds. My hands and forearms would reek of hot bleach water after an hour and a half at the pot sink, and just as the smell finally began to fade, I'd have to go back a couple of days later to do it all again. Seeing—and, worse, smelling—our food prepared killed my appetite. Eggs at breakfast scrambled into a loose, congealed slop. Bacon like semi-raw strips of roadkill. Big cans of green beans heated up to lukewarm, at which temperature they took on the consistency of long, thin tubes of earwax.

A few weeks after this outburst, the Marine flew down to Louisiana again. Very little was said about this trip. He stayed there for three or four days. Since I had resolved not to go home again until the next holiday, when I'd have to, this barely registered. Shortly after this trip, Janelle asked to speak to me on one of those weekly phone calls. The Marine had already said he'd be making a special trip to Durham to see me. Was he on business? I thought she might tell me. Janelle wailed, "It's coming!" into the phone but wouldn't specify what she was talking about. This sort of thing annoyed me. Why imply something bad was about to happen without giving me any information to prepare myself for it?

Sure enough, two days later, he arrived on campus, signed me out, and took me to dinner. The announcement I'd been expecting came before our food did: he and Laura would be separating.

"How do you feel about that, son?" he asked.

What was there to feel? I managed a teenager's shrug. In the past, I had been backhanded and belted too many times for

127

saying what I really thought. Besides, in truth, I didn't even know. What was there to say when I'd seen this moment coming since before I was old enough to read and write? (For what it's worth, I taught myself to write cursive around the age of four and learned how to print sometime later.) That if it meant he'd be moving out of the house, life could only get better? He was desperately trying to have a real connection with me, I think—an authentic father-son moment. There had been a few of those in the past: when he'd gotten up at oh-dark-thirty to make ham biscuits and drive me to morning swim practice; when he'd sucked it up and taken me to see horror movies in my early teens, despite the fact that they scared the crap out of him; when he'd been the calm voice of reason and put a stop to some of Laura's nutty, handsy excesses. If these moments had been the rule and not the exception, I might have had more to say, but a lifetime of inspiring ill-concealed disgust (no matter how many times he and Laura proclaimed they were proud of me) forms an arc that only bends in one direction.

Once we'd run out of things to say, he took me to the mall for parental guilt-shopping. He bought me a trench coat I had been wanting and a couple of shirts. Afterward, the supermarket: snacks, ramen noodles, bread, sandwich meat, Pepsi. In other words, the stuff I was increasingly living on since the cafeteria food was disgusting.

Back in the room, the bitter laughter came. I'm not sure who else was there. Paul. Probably Alex, who'd grown up in Grifton, maybe half an hour away from Greenville. He had a no-fucks-given streak of cynicism as sharp and as dark as obsidian. It matched mine and may have surpassed it. Palmer might have been there too. He was utterly uninterested in the rules and had the benefit of several older siblings to help him break them without detection.

"So my parents are splitting up."

"Dude," Paul said. "That's hurtin'."

"You don't know the half of it."

I thought about the Marine driving back to Greenville alone in his little white Datsun hatchback, maybe listening to the radio and changing stations when the ones in the Raleigh-Durham area faded out. More probably, he drove in silence, maybe grinding his teeth. He didn't seem to like music, but then, he was hard of hearing and couldn't perceive it clearly. By the time he got home, Janelle would be in bed. Laura too, most likely. I had a feeling he'd knock himself out with a few glasses of scotch on the rocks, his usual poison. In an odd way, I felt awful for him. Anguish was a new entry in his visible emotional repertoire, which had previously consisted only of a grim numbness and varying degrees of rage. In his anguish, he seemed to want me to be more upset than I was, to share it with him, but then, he had always wanted things from me that I couldn't give; he had always demanded that I be someone I wasn't. More than that, Janelle and I had never really known him. No questions about Vietnam, no talk of the past, no extended family to fill in the gaps. We were basically forbidden to talk to him. I never told Paul or Palmer or Alex about the day he picked me up and threw me in the pond, screaming *"You've ruined him! You've ruined him!"* at Laura before stalking into the house to sulk in his chair and drink himself numb. That night, I felt as sorry as I could. But beyond that, there was nothing to feel except a faint twinge of anticipatory relief at the prospect of life becoming less horrible, maybe.

That, of course, is not how things worked out.

CHAPTER 14: THE SCENIC ROUTE

Our Christmas trip that year would be our last one together as a family. The Marine and Laura made one of their "it'll be good for the children" executive decisions: they opted for a scenic-route itinerary that would add a couple of days to the drive down to Louisiana, thinking we'd be so amazed by it that we'd overlook the uncomfortable reality of spending that much extra time in a station wagon that smelled like sour milk, but they neglected to mention it until we were in the car and thoroughly sick of each other. Borrowing Granny's floaty station wagon again (the Datsuns weren't big enough and our big Mercury sedan was a gas hog), we drove south via Atlanta, crossed Alabama via Birmingham and Tuscaloosa, and took the historic Natchez Trace Parkway across the southern half of Mississippi. From there, we had to double back via Baton Rouge to get to New Orleans. Although the scenery along the parkway was as green and lovely as one would expect, we'd grown up in the livid South and were not awed by antebellum homes and Spanish moss. While pretty, the scenery we passed wasn't exactly novel or different. Annoyed, the Marine barked at us for not taking in more of the sights as we passed by, for seeming not to care.

"Are we supposed to be looking out the window for six hours straight?" I asked, cross at the prospect of spending another day in the goddamn car.

He remained grim, Laura kept desperately trying to feign good cheer while screaming on the inside, and Janelle was, as usual, checked out and bumping. For some reason, I couldn't seem to slide into my own private Idaho of blankness this time. The present kept rasping against me. I'd already looked at the road atlas, seen how far out of the way we were going, and shuddered in claustrophobic despair. Later, when I brought up the craziness of the route we were taking, Laura heaved a sigh and said, "We just wanted to make it *special* for you and your sister."

On our final night before arriving in New Orleans, we stopped at a hotel in Natchez, at the end of the parkway. The tension in the car had grown unbearable, making even a crappy roadside hotel an oasis of sorts. The Marine was doing most of the driving but talking very little, only opening his mouth when something annoyed him enough to make him break his vow of silence. I was tired of it, of him, of her, of the whole trip, and we weren't even in Louisiana yet. (Remember: the correct pronunciation is "Looziana.")

"Are you and your dad going to bunk in together?" Laura asked, having cornered me by the car as we were unloading it. She was more googly-eyed than usual and flashing a too-bright smile. Pills. I saw the desperation on her face and heard it in her voice. She embodied every writerly cliché about eyes pleading with you, not to mention a few mental-health ones from the DSM about boundaries and age-appropriateness.

"He's your husband, not mine," I said, appalled, and walked away.

The next morning, we started the last leg of the trip at oh-dark-thirty. This time, the parental flair for good intentions divorced from pragmatic essentials like communication and logic kind of paid off: they wanted us to arrive in the French Quarter early enough to have breakfast at the Café du Monde. Props for getting things right occasionally. The Marine drove around and found a secured parking lot. Walking through the Quarter, I went slack-jawed in awe at how *different* the city was from anywhere else I'd ever been. I kept tripping on the cobblestone streets because I was gawking at the old Spanish buildings and not looking where I was going. The exuberance of the façades, painted pink and blue and butterscotch, was a welcome contrast after North Carolina's drab ranch houses and red-brick Federal architecture. New Bern's Swiss heritage and its status as the former state capital had left it with plenty of wrought iron and old buildings, but compared to the French Quarter that first morning, New Bern's finest added up to a few blocks of small-town quaintness (the fire hydrants downtown were painted to look like historical figures, and Laura's favorite was the one she called "Betsy Ross with the leaking boobs") at a right angle to the riverfront and not much more. What clinched it for me, though, was a boy. White, maybe seventeen or eighteen, good-looking. No, make that *very* good-looking. Earrings, snappy clothes, probably stumbling home from a club with a couple of friends. My nascent gaydar started clicking. The three of them passed by, no doubt disregarding the punch-drunk Moores as being just another family of yawning tourists from some flat tragedy of a state like Nebraska. *I belong here*, I thought. I had felt the same thing upon visiting NCSSM for the first time. This was a *city*, though, and one I even had ties to. There are a few memories in life that burn themselves onto the screen behind your eyes, forever available for future viewing. Even if the colors and details fade with time, the shapes and outlines are indelible. That morning in New Orleans was one of the good ones.

We spent the rest of the morning walking around the Quarter, riding the streetcar into the Garden District to look at the mansions, ducking into shops to get out of the dense heat. The Marine wouldn't let me buy some records (OMD this time, a couple of singles and remixes from *Junk Culture* and *Architecture & Morality*) I found in a shop and was desperate to own, insisting that I come back and bargain for a lower price. That was how things worked in the French Quarter, he said. You haggled. He knew how to pronounce the odd street names, too: Ursulines, Tchoupitoulas, Carondelet. The "Royal" in Royal Street had two syllables, stress on the second. A new emotion of my own began to simmer underneath this touristic limerence: resentment. We'd had a family connection to this place all my life and I was just now seeing it for the first time at age fifteen? We could have been eating jambalaya and seafood gumbo and shrimp étouffée instead of Laura's flavorless pork chops and syrupy-sweet canned corn?

Later in the day, we returned to the car and drove west out of the city proper into the suburb of Kenner, where the Marine's younger cousin Janet—Loretta's daughter—had a townhouse near Lake Pontchartrain. A sharp redhead in her thirties, she seemed to take our measure at once. Unlike the Marine and Laura, she talked to Janelle and me as if we were actual people, not swirling space objects to be measured by our distance from parental expectations. Nor was there any implicit begging us to act like little children again, eyes wide open and seeing nothing, doting on her in her loneliness. With Janelle, Janet disappeared into the bedroom for a time, for some girl talk that presumably did not entail mandatory panties-off twat-maintenance lessons.

With me, she was pretty hands-off, a welcome (and literal) change from Laura's grabby desperation.

After a few days in New Orleans, we drove west to Lafayette, in the heart of Cajun country. Loretta didn't live in a bayou, just a ranch house in the suburbs. There, we passed a couple of completely unmemorable days before heading north to Ball, the suburb of Alexandria where the Marine had grown up and most of his family still lived. We'd be staying with his cousin Albert. Albert and his wife had two teenage sons, Darren and Keith. I couldn't get my head around it: all these people named Moore, and we hadn't known they existed three months ago. In the case of Darren and Keith, I think it had been more like three *weeks*.

Albert ran a shoe store. It may have been in the family for some time. When Janelle and I were very young, the Marine used to lecture us about education. The shoe-store horror story tended to precede his end-of-the-day "Find a way to work for yourself" rants. This earlier version went "You have to do well so that you never have to work in a shoe store all day, smelling other people's feet. You don't make any money and no one respects you. It's the most disgusting job in the world. Never do that." The day we arrived, we met Albert at the store. Keith was in the local high school marching band, and there had been a parade in town that day; afterward, he and some friends would be stopping by to meet us.

Janelle and I already looked very out of place with our '80s peroxide and baubles and curls. I didn't own boots and flannel back then (the couple of years I spent in Portland and Seattle in my mid 30s would result in a top-to-bottom wardrobe overhaul), and now that I could take out the starter stud in my left earlobe, I preferred earrings that dangled. We sat in the stockroom doing polite nods and smiles and feeling like long-limbed Martians who'd just beamed down from a spaceship. As with the other visits, the grownups left the room to talk in hushed voices. Finally, Keith and his friends (four white boys, one black) burst into the stockroom and made straight for the vending machine. It was the old-fashioned kind, basically a refrigerator with a coin box and a bottle-opener mounted on the door. Introductions were made; glass Coke bottles were popped open; and then the five trooped out again to put away their instruments and change out of their band uniforms.

After they left, Albert stormed into the stockroom. "Did you *see* that?" he snapped at us.

Janelle and I looked at each other.

"See what?" I asked. Had one of the kids stolen something? They didn't pay for their Cokes, but when your dad owns the store, isn't the occasional soft drink one of the perks?

"That little [redacted] boy coming in here and helping himself to a Coke just like he was as good as the rest of 'em."

Silence fell, a cold and sudden eclipse in the conversation. To the Marine's credit, his lips disappeared into a straight white line. In a rare moment of absolute, horrified unity, Janelle and I exchanged a "what the fuck did he just say?" look. To say we hadn't been brought up in a racist environment would be an outright lie. It was the South. I remember being driven to school in the second grade by the principal's husband. Finished with his Styrofoam cup of coffee, he tossed it out the window of his truck. When I objected, he said, "It's okay. It gives [redacted] s jobs." Laura's family reunions down in Hyde County and Little Washington could be just as bad: the [redacted]s this, the [redacted]s that, and you can't even walk down the street in Miami anymore because of all the goddamn Cubans. The

Marine and Laura did not use those words (the redacted one starts with N), and we were told not to.

The transition from paper-white Carolina Country Day into the Greenville's public schools had been racially scary at first. A few black guys in my PE class pushed me around that first year, then apparently lost interest. On the other hand, the black girls in my classes were the only people who were consistently nice to me. Many of them were two years older and had been held back by a system set up to keep them down. They got it, and often displayed a graciousness that white adults three times their age tended to lack. At one point during that first year, a rumor went around that I was racist. Someone had asked if I had any black friends. I said no, because at my old school, there had only been one or two, but they never stayed for more than a year. It wasn't that I was a racist, I just had never had the chance to get to know any black kids. This of course was taken out of context, turned into a middle-school kerfuffle, and died out when the next tweenage scandal hit the rumor mill. I was horrified that people might think of me that way. Given that I was already designated as a faggot and therefore subhuman, the last fucking thing I needed was to be hated for an additional reason.

Now this. The moment passed. I wish we'd spoken up. Perhaps Albert realized we didn't share his Stars-and-Bars views on race relations. I didn't ask. Somebody changed the subject, and before long it was time to drive back to their house for dinner. In college, Janelle and I visited Ball one more time, and enough years have passed that I can't separate the very little that happened on the first visit from the very little that happened on the second. Suffice to say, there wasn't much to do in Greater Alexandria. A few days passed, I read some books and listened to some music, and before long, it was time to load Granny's station wagon up again and drive back to New Orleans. Although we could have taken a more direct route back from central Louisiana, I think the Marine and Laura wanted to end the trip on a relatively high note. We stayed one more night in the Big Easy, had a ginormous seafood lunch on our way out (I pissed the Marine off by refusing to peel shrimp with my bare hands but ended up being the only one of us whose fingers didn't stink when we got back in the car), and hit the road.

One last detail of this trip has stayed with me. We drifted through one of the new shopping malls along the Mississippi River in New Orleans, not hunting for anything but passing the time in the way that people do when they've run out of things to say to each other. The Marine and Laura had long been fond of modern Scandinavian furniture, an angular contrast from the heavy, frilly Duncan Phyfe crap Granny had bestowed upon us. The only reason we still had a living room full of it, I had come to understand, was to avoid offending her.

We wandered through tasteful displays of warmly sleek wooden chairs, dining-room tables with tiled surfaces, and sofas that looked as if they didn't absorb oxygen and light. I couldn't seem to get away from Laura. She kept following me; she kept talking at me, desperate babblings about nothing, frantic attempts to engage me in conversations I didn't want to have. Still mulling over everything that had happened on the trip (cousins my age I'd never heard of until a month ago!), I wanted to be alone with my thoughts. Worse, she kept *touching* me. Hands grabbing my shoulders, running down my back, lingering at my butt just one second too long. In the old South, a non-sexual culture of courtly flattery existed between mothers and sons. Among old families (white ones; I doubt this is an

African-American thing, or a Latin one), it may still. There's probably an abhorrent reason underneath this, but I'll leave speculation to the historians and sociologists in the audience. Suffice to say, it probably worked out well enough in families that weren't insane, but it was grossing me out. I literally hissed at her in that Danish furniture shop like a pissed-off cat.

She immediately crumpled in on herself, started crying, and ran away.

A couple of seconds later, the Marine rushed up, shouting: "Why are you hissing at your mother? What the hell are you doing?"

"Tell her to keep her hands off of me," I said.

He didn't get it. And then he did. And then his face froze again in a refusal to acknowledge what he had just heard. Janelle saw it all and got it instantly. She turned up the music on her Walkman, walked away, seated herself in one of the armchairs on the sales floor, and started bumping.

The rest of the way back to North Carolina, I don't anyone spoke beyond the occasional obligatory question whether anyone needed to go to the bathroom when we passed a rest stop.

CHAPTER 15: BLANKS

One Sunday afternoon in early spring, I was waiting for Marci Edwards and her mother to pick me up for the drive back to S&M. They were from Bath, a quaint flyspeck of a town about an hour east of Greenville, halfway to the beach. Settled in the early 1700s, Bath is famous for being North Carolina's oldest town and notorious for being the former home of Edward Teach, the pirate more commonly known as Blackbeard. As for Marci, who was one of my seniors, we were in Latin 2 together but had never really talked until the start of an extended weekend: her ride home fell through at the last minute, and she recognized the dealer logo on Mary's Datsun, convinced the driver of the bus she was on to let her out, ran up to us, and asked if we could give her a ride back as far as Greenville. We said yes, and she ran back inside and called her mother. We're still friends three and a half decades later.

Fast forward to a Sunday afternoon a few months later, the last day of an extended weekend. Laura and I were waiting in the living room. My suitcase was packed and I had a bag of groceries to bring back. Fresh laundry, too. After discovering a bar of soap in one of the washing machines in the campus laundry room, I'd grown leery of washing clothes at school and would save them up when I knew I was going home. As for the Marine, he'd been gone a month already. The weekend he moved out, I had to go back to Greenville to help, passing up the Simple Minds concert Palmer had invited me to. The Marine moved into Granny's little house on Rotary Avenue close to campus, and she moved into a nearby apartment building for senior citizens. Since then, Laura had lost a lot of weight: she looked gaunt, and the dark smudges under her eyes added to the cadaverous effect. The change was shocking. Understandable, but shocking. On those rare, unavoidable weekend/holiday trips back to Greenville, I disappeared into myself almost to the point of forming an event horizon: I stayed in my bedroom with homework or a book, emerging only for meals, and as much as possible attempted to keep her from crying on me. She clutched. She clung. The drinking was a given. The pills were dessert. More than once, it occurred to me that she might get fucked up enough to shoot Janelle and me in our sleep so that we could be together as a family forever, thereby consigning us to hell. Marci and her mom couldn't come soon enough.

Part of that weekend's entertainment had been stalking the Marine. I didn't particularly want to accompany her, but she was too tipsy to be safe behind the wheel. In the mood to bask in self-pity and rage, she gave me directions to a subdivision just outside the city limits, not far from our old house in Avalon. Sure enough, there was the Marine's white Datsun hatchback.

"He's with another woman!" she wailed.

I slowed down.

"Don't stop! They might see us."

"We're in a yellow station wagon. It's the only one in Greenville. We aren't inconspicuous."

"Sometimes you can even see them through the window!"

It didn't occur to me then to ask how she knew this, how

many times she had looked, and whether she thought this knowledge might bring him back.

Now, while we waited for the Edwardses, I was sitting on the floor, resting against the wall. The only things I liked about the room were the sunlight and the soft oyster-grey carpet. The shiny-stiff antique sofa looked nice enough if you were into light-eating furniture but I couldn't stand the thing, and its companion armchair was no less carbuncular. Laura perched on the piano bench.

"He's already with another woman," she said. Why say something once when you can repeat it several times and then have the pleasure of scolding your conversation victim for rolling his eyes?

"Didn't we kind of... establish that?" I wanted to be reading. I wanted to be in Marci's mom's van halfway to Durham, maybe stopping for a Coke at the gas station in Zebulon where everybody stopped when they got off the highway to bypass Raleigh. Back then, stopping for a Coke was a small luxury. Laura wouldn't keep soft drinks in the fridge. Her fear of dentistry (she had gotten six cavities one time when she was a girl, and in a rage, Dick forbade the dentist to use anaesthetic when he filled them) forbade it.

"When he was in Vietnam, I know there were... *other women.*"

Wherever my mind had been, this slapped me back into the present tense. There had been other women more recently than that. We'd walked in on him with one in Atlanta back in the '70s. Having made our way to the hotel from the airport without him there to meet us, we arrived at the room, and there was some other lady. Janelle and I were too young to understand what was happening at the time, but Laura was only too scornfully happy to regale us with the details later. There was also that box of condoms he kept at the ready. "I've had a hysterectomy," Laura pointed out. "It's not as if he needs them."

Back in the present: "What?" I strained to hear the sound of tires on the driveway, an engine shutting off.

"In Vietnam... when he got back, that's when I got pregnant with you. You know we had been trying to have children for a long time."

I hoped she wouldn't start on this tangent—any version of it—again. Although we weren't high-born enough in the gynecocracy of the Old South to be obsessed with breeding and family lines, Laura loved few things as much as talking about her womb-related failures and achievements. One of her favorites was the story of the Miraculous Conception, A.K.A. me. They'd been trying to get pregnant for years. It kept not happening. I believe there were a few miscarriages before me (plus, between me and Janelle, a boy who came close enough to term to be named Paul Wahab), although those details waxed and waned depending on how much Taylor Lake Country White she'd consumed that evening. I didn't really want to know but I felt I had to listen. After all, no teenager wants to imagine their parents having sex. On the whole, I'd have been happier if my creation myth (or reality, come to think of it) had been a *Brave New World* lullaby involving a test tube and an incubator. Laura was certain that their fertility-related difficulties were a result of the Marine's dysfunctional sperm. As a fighter pilot, he'd been subjected to extreme temperatures and pressures. Not to put too fine a point on it, he and the other men in his squadron were mostly shooting blanks.

The night I became pregnant with you, I knew right away, went the backstory. *A woman knows: there's a special spark. You know it.*

It's a mystical event.

Naturally, enough was never enough: *Every other pilot in his squadron, their wives were having girls. And that's if they could even get pregnant at all. We thought you were going to be a girl too. When the doctors showed us your little ding-dong, we were so proud! The first boy in his squadron!*

O irony.

"But when I became pregnant with you, I started experiencing... symptoms. Something wasn't right. I went to the doctor and got checked out, and... I had a *disease.*" Her face crumpled. "He brought me a *disease* back from Vietnam. It was chlamydia."

She collected herself. I sat as still as I could. Where the *fuck* were Marci and her mother?

"Everyone tried to convince me to have an abortion, but we'd been trying for so long, I wouldn't do it. I just took the antibiotics and prayed you'd be okay."

Sometimes, there just aren't words. I suppose in this case others might feel incredible gratitude, the burning rush of a bullet whizzing past the head and missing, but my feelings on the matter are a little more delicate and nuanced. In the pro-choice/pro-life debate, I'm very clear on where I stand. None of this had ever been necessary and all of it could have been avoided.

"You don't get chlamydia from shaking hands!" Laura wailed.

Just as she broke down, my ride came. She pulled herself together enough to see me to the door, and I was able to escape for another couple of months.

Sometimes when you can't talk about something, it's enough to be quietly near the right person. Marci was one of the few people I could have been around after that without just melting into a mass of inchoate screaming. She knew when to ask questions and when not to, and was kind enough not to pry. The mists rolled in again, and the whole trip back to campus and quite a bit of time afterward is simply gone now.

Back at school, I went through the motions. When I could remember to, I performed intelligence and attentiveness and acted as if I were capable of giving a shit. To be honest, it wasn't always doom and gloom. One night, some friends of mine set up a boombox in the in the glass breezeway that connected Beall and Bryan and blasted the Violent Femmes (mainly "Add It Up" and "Blister in the Sun" on endless repeat). We danced/moshed/spun around/whatever until one of the residential advisors came along and chased us away. Around then, I smoked weed for the first time with a couple of friends who shall remain nameless. Nothing really happened (it never does, the first time) but I was glad for the chance to corrupt myself. A trip over to NC State in Raleigh involved the consumption of rivers of Ernest & Julio Gallo Chablis on empty stomachs. This was my first time getting stumbling drunk, my first time lying on the floor and watching the room spin around me, my first time puking up a gutful of cheap wine. I grossed Paul out and got in trouble a couple of days later when Roland, the 2nd Wyche RA, overheard me talking about it with someone. Then there was the time a couple of guys (I think William Hendrix was in on it) on my hall and I played a prank (it was my idea) on Cyrus Erickson, the buff ROTC guy who lived across from Paul and me. He was taking a shower, and somebody had a big plastic cooler with a spigot after some sports event or other. We filled it up and carried it carefully into the toilet stall next to the shower. Then one of us pressed the button, sending a strong stream of water into the commode. It sounded like the longest piss in history. We started cracking up when Cyrus asked who it was, what was going on. Then he shocked us by walking out of the shower naked to see for himself. It wasn't the outcome I had in mind, but… no objections.

It's bizarre to write about my time at what was then considered (and still seems to be) the best high school in the United States when I have so little memory of being in class. For one thing, by this point in my junior year, I often wasn't. I was at the mall or on 9th Street. Some days, I just couldn't be bothered, so I took walks. In addition to everything else that was going on with me, an ugly truth about S&M had become clear: we'd been misled about our prospects after graduation. Since the school was so new and there were no other ones like it in the country, universities didn't distinguish between it and our old high schools. In other words, those of us who had been getting straight As back in Normalton, North Carolina and were now getting Bs and Cs as we'd been warned during orientation that we would, could largely forget about Stanford and the Ivy League. Admissions officers didn't make the leap of logic that we were still those same straight-A students, and after two years in that pressure-cooker of a school, we could handle anything college threw at us. Carolina would generally take us, and so would NC State, both very good schools but not in the same league as Harvard and Yale. There was Duke if you were rich and preppy enough to want to go there, which I wasn't. S&M's administration had made a few overtures to address the problem: they abolished the GPA system, for example. In theory, it wasn't a bad idea; in practice, it turned out to be problematic: it meant we had to leave that part of our applications blank, sometimes resulting in rejections.

There was one more thing I was too embarrassed to talk

about: I actually had no idea how the college-application process was supposed to work. University brochures started arriving about halfway through junior year. Most went to my home address, but a few turned up in my NCSSM mailbox. There were the usual suspects: Carolina, State, Duke, Appalachian, Western Carolina, UNC-Greensboro. A few private colleges I don't remember now. For some reason I got one from Oberlin, one of the few I had heard of. I held onto that one. The thing was, college was supposed to be a decision you made with family input. I didn't have a family, I had factions. What was I actually supposed to *do*? With Stanford and the Ivies off the table now that my straight As and the swim team were history, how the hell was I supposed to choose? Who would even take me? I overheard people talking about college visits, but the Marine and Laura were too busy barking, weeping, drinking, and bickering to be of much help. Besides, neither of them had the life experience to be helpful: he had dropped out of Texas A&M to join the military and she had started college in adulthood. They didn't have social lives, so there were no friends they could ask. How many schools was I supposed to apply to? How did I narrow it down? And when the time came, where was the money for the applications supposed to come from? I never spoke up about this because in that environment I worried it would be tantamount to admitting I didn't know how to do something really basic like boiling water or tying my shoelaces.

The logical thing would have been to grit my teeth, redouble my efforts, pull my grades up, and apply only to colleges far enough away from Greenville that flights would be required. I did try. More than once. But it's hard to feel rescued and ripped off at the same time, especially when every call and letter from home brings a fresh load of insanity with it. Now the Marine and Laura were arguing about money. He resented paying child support. On Laura's secretary's salary, she could hardly afford to pay her own bills, much less support the two of us, and resented him for resenting it. Neither of them seemed to notice that Janelle was now stoned most of the time (and, at the age of 13, still bumping when she wasn't taking one of her hours-long naps). She had turned into that angry kid who sits in the back of the class next to an open window and tokes up from a one-hitter when the teacher leaves the room. She was dropping acid, too, which I somehow knew and they didn't. At dinner, sometimes she just pushed the food around on her plate and stared at blue puppies and pink kittens that weren't there. The Marine had lapsed back to barking orders and threats at me: *bring your grades up, get a girlfriend, straighten up and fly right, get a girlfriend, don't piss this away or I'm gonna jerk you out of there and make you come back here and live with me...* I fell back into my old habit of holding the phone away from my head far enough that his ranting sounded like an argument between a bee and a wasp. Now and then I even hung up on him. Hollowed out and bordering on despair at times, I had no idea what to do. When I was with friends who would listen, I droned on at times. There were a lot of late nights with Palmer in the Wyche basement watching MTV until four in the morning. He would prop the door open and smoke even though we weren't supposed to.

"Alcohol's okay, but sometimes I just prefer smoking," he said one night, lighting up. "It's more destructive. Want one?"

I tried one. It was terrible. So much for cigarettes. I'd take my draughts of blankness elsewhere, thanks but no thanks.

CHAPTER 16: THE CHILL OF LATE SPRING

The night before prom, I stayed at Steve Zung's house, as I had done for the last six or seven weeks in a row. Steve was a local Durham guy, not an S&M student. Half Chinese, half white Canadian, and in Durham because his father, a prominent psychiatrist, taught at Duke. I met Steve off campus at a play put on by a local theater company. We hit it off and talked until our friends dragged us away; a few days later, he stopped by NCSSM to see if he could find me. He did: we bumped into each other in front of Hill.

"What are you doing here?" I asked, shocked.

"Looking for you. Want to go somewhere?"

I probably had a pile of homework. Having concluded that Cs and low Bs would not do, I'd redoubled my efforts to pull my grades up. But when the cool interesting Eurasian guy you've just met goes to the trouble of driving across town (back in the days before cell phones and texting, this was a big deal) to hang out, other priorities assert themselves. Steve drove a copper-brown, tank-like SUV from the '70s and had named it Diane, which made him seem even cooler, although I couldn't have explained why I felt that way. (In retrospect, it's obvious: I had an instant crush on him. He could have named his car Diarrhea and I'd still have swooned.) So we drove around, got burgers somewhere on Ninth Street, talked with the scalding intensity that teenagers have when they feel everything keenly but know next to nothing. I had to be on campus again by eight (I don't even think I signed out), although this mattered a bit less in Wyche. Located on the eastern edge of campus, my dorm was convenient for after-dark sneaking. You could run in shadows most of the way from Broad Street to the basement door with the broken lock, and usually get back inside without getting caught.

Steve invited me to stay at his house that weekend. I should eat some real food, he said. And I would like his younger sister and brother, Kathi and Patrick. Originally from China, Dr. Zung was usually either at work or in his home office. Now and then, there would be a sighting: he'd pass by, look at me as if he couldn't quite figure out who I was and why I was there, and scowl. He made me nervous, and when I later learned he had developed important assessment tools for depression and anxiety, I was not the least bit surprised. In any case, I'm not sure he ever actually knew my name. He didn't seem to mind me being there, or if he did, he kept his opinion to himself; in the weeks that followed, the Zungs more or less adopted me.

Steve would usually stop by after school once or twice a week, and we'd either hang out in my room or leave campus. Some of these excursions got complicated; sometimes Kathi and Patrick would come along. We went all the way out to Jordan Lake one night because their guidance counselor Mr. Morgan, the kind you sometimes become friends with outside of school, had a house out there. Steve got his first speeding ticket racing to get me back to campus before curfew that time.

Other students started to notice how much time I was

spending with him off campus. Although no one came right out and asked if Steve was my boyfriend, I could tell people thought so. It was in the way they talked about him with me. A look, a tone of voice, a slight hesitation: I could connect the dots. In a weird way, this horrified me and made me proud at the same time. There were a couple of problems, though: he was (and is) straight, I was crazy about him (on top of my baseline level of crazy), and I still hadn't actually come out yet.

My feelings for him were almost as intense as my denial. Even though I knew I was gay, it was the kind of admission that could only seep out under the crack of the door I'd slammed shut in my mind. I knew it was true and was desperate for it not to be. Perhaps more than that, I needed the monsters to be wrong about me. Honesty looked like capitulation, the most depressing and sordid kind imaginable. I'd be a filthy pariah with sperm in my throat and shit on my dick. As this carnival gyre of lunacy spun around in my head, I told myself he was straight and so was I and we'd both find girlfriends, and yet somehow I also began to recognize my inability to feel that giddy, scorching incandescence toward a girl. I talked about him nonstop and bored everyone I knew except, perhaps, Sarah Lund, the guidance counselor who was doing her best to manage my lunacy.

Weirded out yet? There's more. For example: I *wasn't* having sexual fantasies about him. I know how that sounds. Despite being able to do advanced math in my head, I wasn't putting two and two together. I wasn't spanking the monkey to fantasies of doing *that* with him. (Or to fantasies of doing anything else with anybody else, for that matter: being told all your life that you're under constant telepathic surveillance kind of puts a damper on the urge to jerk off.) Despite having had the process of sucking a cock explained to me in the most explicit of terms, I'd never even hinted that I might want to do that with him. It literally hadn't occurred to me. The old shame and mockery walled off the idea. That's how the closet works. Yet I also had moments of clarity, in spite of myself: I knew that if he were to make the first move, I would happily—ecstatically—go along with it and do whatever he wanted.

I dreaded prom and didn't want to go. If it was going to be anything like Cotillion, an annual dance for Greenville's white high school students, I wanted none of it. When you're not one of the Cool Kids, no one will dance with you (which is just as well, since you're unlikely to know how) and you hang out on the bleachers with your fellow social riffraff. When you're one of the Designated School Fags, you also have to hope that no one will punch you in the face, pour a drink on you, or gather a crowd of jeering thugs to call you names. But in keeping with my lifelong inability to realize I sometimes have other options, I resigned myself to going. There was that terrible run-up interval a few weeks ahead of time: students started asking each other out; rumors spread like hemorrhagic fevers. In the end, I double-dated with Carrie Floyd, Becky Collins, and Floyd Bullard. I was sort of dating Carrie, whom I'm certain knew I was gay but thought I was interesting enough to keep around. (Interestingly, Floyd has also come out since then, and he now teaches math at S&M.)

The Saturday of the prom, I spent the afternoon at the Zungs', getting ready. Steve drove me around to pick up my tux (white, with a teal cummerbund, it only sort of worked because it was the eighties and would have been a sartorial disaster in any other decade) and the corsage and all the other formalities. The Marine had been only too happy to cover the cost of all this. If it would make me straight, he'd have cheerfully taken out a second mortgage. What I really wanted to do was ditch the whole mess and go somewhere with Steve, like the house at Jordan Lake, just us. But Becky's parents had rented a limousine and someone else had made reservations at one of those Japanese steakhouses with teppanyaki tables.

That first part of the evening went as well as it could. Back on campus, the four of us piled into the limo when it arrived, stumbling through conversation that would have flowed if we'd been wearing our usual jeans and T-shirts. At dinner, the chef at the next table flipped a shrimp onto my lapel, staining it. Mercifully, I could hide the oily splotch under the corsage, but I worried about having to pay an extra laundry fee later. At the prom, which was held in the ballroom at a hotel in downtown Durham, we danced our obligatory few dances and drifted apart. It was all exactly what you'd expect: wood-paneled walls, big inexpensive bouquets of pale roses and sprays of baby's breath, and that awful Phil Collins vengeance dirge "In the Air Tonight" as a theme. Put a couple hundred socially awkward smart kids in uncomfortable tuxes and gowns and the hormone-laced smell of teenage anxiety will thicken the air to an almost pudding-like texture. I have never liked pudding. I liked Carrie, Becky, and Floyd well enough. I couldn't leave soon enough. I had been under the impression Steve would be picking me up later that night, and when he didn't show, I started to panic. For the first time, I understood what it meant to be alone in a crowd. It did not, of course, occur to me that calling the Zungs' home in the middle of the night looking for him would not endear me to his parents.

Eventually, Steve did show up, mumbling apologies as he drove us back to his house. Relief pushed back the despair, but in the days and weeks that followed, even my supernatural powers of self-deception weren't enough to shield me from the obvious chill in the air. He called and stopped by campus less often. When we talked, his mind went somewhere else. I'd spent enough time tuning other people out to know what being ignored looked like.

"Have I done something?" I asked him one weekend afternoon. We were sitting in the hammock in his back yard talking. "I'm worried... about our relationship."

This felt like a very adult thing to say, and on some level I was proud of myself for putting it like that. At the same time, it also felt very wrong, as if I'd pushed a button and started a countdown timer.

"It's nothing," he said. "Mr. Morgan once said growth is hard. It's like you expand, but once you're bigger, you feel hollow on the inside. It takes time for your insides to grow to fill in the new empty space. That's how I feel most of the time now."

"Oh," I said, getting it but not wanting to. "I think I feel like that too sometimes."

In truth, this was an understatement. My parents' separation hadn't made anything better. Almost from the moment the Marine had announced his intention to leave, the fighting started. They dragged me home for the Big Family Talk about custody. The Marine wanted us to live with him. The idea was so absurd that Janelle and I couldn't hide our shock, although to our credit, I think we did try.

Turning him down hurt him deeply, and when he demanded to know why, things went from... well, what are the comparatives and superlatives when you're already in hell? Which Jacuzzi full of boiling sulfur reeks less?

"Look how you've treated us?" I managed to say.

Shouting ensued: We only loved him for his money. If we thought he was a child-abuser, we should just call Child Protective Services on him and be done with it. None of us loved him. Laura had turned us against him, and one day we'd be old enough to see that. (On that last point, he wasn't entirely wrong.) He stormed out of the kitchen, out of the house, and sped away. It was not until later, in the shaken and very quiet aftermath (the silence only broken by the rhythmic thuds from Janelle's disintegrating armchair as she bumped herself into oblivion), did it occur to me that he was the one who brought up child abuse, not us. Back to school I went the next day. O glorious blankness.

This was the backdrop. It's the reason I practically moved in with the Zungs. There were tensions but the lack of actual screaming was a welcome relief.

At times, overwhelmed by the things I couldn't name and the things that I could, I would simply stay in bed crying. One afternoon Paul came back to our room and found me like that; he went and got Roland, our hall advisor, to come talk to me. Nothing either of them said made a difference. Nothing could have. I couldn't tell anyone what was really going on. As Steve retreated and the school year drew to its close, I vanished into myself, resigned to going back to a home that didn't feel like home, with people I cared about very much and wanted never to see again if it could somehow be arranged.

CHAPTER 17: WHAT I GOT AWAY WITH, WHAT I GOT AWAY FROM

Laura had downsized. With the Marine gone and me away at NCSSM and presumably going to college after that, there was no reason to stay in the house on King George Road. In fairness, I liked the new place over on Ragsdale. In a neighborhood that managed to be suburban and central at the same time, it was a three-bedroom, two-bath ranch house with good built-ins. The large screened back porch around back would be shady and comfortable for much of the year, and there was a new ceiling fan in every room. The master bedroom had a vast walk-in closet and bathroom suite. This would become Laura's home office. Janelle got the larger of the two bedrooms. She complained about the forest-green walls, which was to be expected: she was only happy when she had something or someone to hate. The room I ended up with, well, let's just say I was used to being in closets. I didn't like having to share a bathroom with Janelle, who would bang on the door and bellow "shit faster!" if I stayed in there too long, but I understood that our previous luxuries were now outside of the post-family price range.

The only thing that made the prospect of summer bearable, at least at first, was the Zungs' invitation to spend a week with them at the beach in mid-June. They had rented hotel rooms down at Emerald Isle, and they seemed to want me around. Plans were made: the Steve would stop in Greenville on the way down from Durham, pick me up, and we'd meet Kathi and Patrick—who would travel with their father—at the motel.

As soon as Steve arrived to pick me up (if you've read the Harry Potter books or seen the films, the scene in which the Weasley brothers rescue Harry with the flying car has a sweet, stinging resonance), it was obvious he had checked out. Minimal conversation in the car (not Diane this time but a white Chevrolet hatchback I hadn't seen before). There were grumbles and speeding. Scary maneuvers. I understood what our friendship was and what it wasn't, or at least I told myself I did. I needed every second I spent riding shotgun listening to him vent even as his lack of a deeper interest shredded me from the inside out.

There had always been a sort of ritual quality to driving to the beach, a subtle progression as the coastal plain flattened out and the color of the sky intensified. Inland, in Greenville, humidity could turn the sky into a dense concrete haze at the height of summer, but east of New Bern, the Atlantic kept the firmament blue. The trees would change too, deciduous ones giving way to expanses of loblolly pines. The first tang of ocean salt in the air; the shops selling boats, bait, and tackle; the signs along the highway pointing out the shrinking number of miles to Morehead City and Atlantic Beach: normally these would lift the spirits. This time, I felt a sense of mounting dread as we drove east. He was driving like a lunatic.

It turned out to be justified. We got in a wreck just outside of Morehead, the last town before the big bridge connecting the mainland coast with the barrier islands that comprise the Outer Banks. It was just a fender-bender—Steve misjudged traffic in a turn lane and rear-ended the car head of us—and neither of us was hurt, but the Chevy's headlights and front bumper were smashed. There would be no way to get them fixed before the Zungs returned to Durham the following week, which meant we wouldn't be able to go anywhere at night.

This did not help Steve's mood.

Dinner that night—at what might have been the only Chinese restaurant in Morehead—was a pu-pu tray of tension, unvoiced anger, and the stench of primordial cooking oil. Dr. Zung was at the beach for a conference and would be there all week, staying in a separate room, there but not spending time with the kids (which was how they/we wanted it anyway). Steve was embarrassed for me to see his dad mad at him, angry at the world, and all I could do was shut up and disappear into myself, skills I'd long since mastered and still seemed to need. I didn't belong there, but there was nowhere else I wanted to be, nowhere else I could go.

What do you do at the beach for a week when there's not much to do? Swim. Sunbathe. Swim some more. Read. Take long walks. Eat. Swim. Sleep. The hotel, one of those low-rise beachfront affairs from the '50s, offered tragic amenities. A dire café that served runny eggs at breakfast and soggy burgers at lunch, a sad rec room with a few out-of-date videogames and a pool table, a couple of shelves of paperbacks softening to pulp in the humidity. There was nothing nearby. Down the beach, a massive pier jutted quite far out into the ocean. Lights on it suggested festivities, amusements, glimmers of nightlife. On our last night at the beach, we decided to walk to that pier, however long it might take. It might have been a couple of miles away, although with no landmarks nearby for scale, we couldn't gauge the distance. The three of us (Steve having gone off somewhere to bask in his angst) hiked until we were dripping with sweat, and the pier seemed to retreat ahead of us. Eventually we gave up and turned back, fearing it would be three a.m. if we tried to walk the whole way.

Having given up on the pier but too energized from the walk to want to go to sleep yet, the three of us ended up in the rec room. I fed one of the games (Space Invaders, I think, or Galaga) a quarter and it stuck halfway down.

"Hey! This thing took my money!" An idea came to me. "Help me turn this thing upside down? I think we can get my quarter to fall out."

The games were the tabletop kind, not the upright arcade machines, so this idea wasn't as nutty as it might sound. Torpor broken, Kathi and Patrick got up and helped out. It worked, too: my quarter fell out. So did the rest of them.

"Oh shit," I said, looking at the pile of change. To a broke high school student in the '80s, it was a lot of money, maybe $30. I looked around at the other machines. "Are you guys thinking what I'm thinking?"

Turns out, they were. When one game wouldn't give up its contents, I brazenly walked down to the front office, smiled, and asked for a screwdriver.

"I've got something that needs screwing," I said, beaming charm. When you have curly blond hair, you can get away with anything. "I promise I'll bring it right back."

Sometime during our act of petty larceny, Steve wandered in, took one look at the upside-down game we were plundering, said "I want nothing to do with this," and stalked out.

Shrugs all around. We divided the money, which came to about $60 each, and after I put my stash of quarters in my suitcase, I took the screwdriver back to the front desk, beamed, and said thank you.

That night, I couldn't sleep, half because of my Steve-related anxieties (and what they meant) and half because the Marine had decreed that Janelle and I were to go on a four-day sailing trip with him. He would be there to pick us up a couple of hours after I got back from Atlantic Beach. The one time I'd ever been sailing, the boom cracked me across the head when we turned, almost knocking me into the water. The Marine had warned me about it and assumed his job was done. Having no idea what he was talking about, I wasn't on the lookout; I didn't expect a metal rod with a sail attached to it to come pivoting at my head. With my predilection for head injuries, it was remarkable that I got a bruise and not a concussion, but then, I also wasn't taken to the hospital for an X-ray. Now we were going to have to spend four *days* on a boat with him?

I did *not* want to go. Neither did Janelle. What the hell was there to look forward to? "Together as a family" time? That ship had sailed. A weekend of awkwardness and nausea, more like. Puking over the side if the seas got rough. The Marine barking orders, coarsening up as he did around his sailing-buddy friends when the beer was flowing. Talk of when I was going to find a girlfriend, had I gotten laid yet, and if so, how did I like pussy. This was veering too close to earlier threats or promises from both parents to take me to a whore when I was old enough. Janelle would be my single link to sanity amid all of this. Maybe with her there, they'd hold back on all the vulgar talk, or maybe not. It's not that I objected to the vulgarity, by the way. I just didn't like being the *subject* of it. Humor at my awkwardness, my ineptitude at being a boy. There would be jokes at my expense, a slight (or not so slight) mocking of my too-formal speech and my clumsy discomfort. The Marine's friends' sons seemed more relaxed in their own skins, and their father-son chemistry seemed more natural. They acted like buddies; we acted like people whose only shared language was one studied for a couple of semesters back in high school, ages ago. Cram all of this psychological torture into the small confines of a large sailboat, and someone was going to end up in the water.

I'd been home all of two hours, procrastinating, morose, when the Marine showed up. He demanded to know why I hadn't packed.

"He just got here," Laura said.

"We have to get on the road!" the Marine spluttered.

"I don't want to," I said.

He exploded into a dark torrent of the same indignities he spewed the day Janelle and I refused to move in with him: I never wanted to do anything with him, I didn't care about anything he enjoyed, I was selfish, and so on. Laura rolled her eyes. Janelle figured into this somewhere, but as usual she was overlooked amid all the furor surrounding my failure to be exactly what someone else expected.

I wanted to retreat into the nest I'd made in my walk-in closet in our previous house: beanbag chair covered with a sleeping bag, small bookshelf, reading lamp. I wanted to grab a book, a Coke and some potato chips, and vanish for the rest of the weekend. My current bedroom wasn't much bigger, and would do. If I could read one book after another, I wouldn't have to think about how Steve had spent the whole week blowing me off. All I could do was keep out of his way and wait to be flicked aside at the end of the week.

He dropped me off and didn't even come inside.

I didn't cry, but it took effort.

In less than ten minutes, the Marine barking orders the

160

whole time, Janelle and I were in his car and heading east toward Belhaven. Most of the way to Little Washington, the Marine kept the conversation on life support. We had nothing to talk about, though, and by the time we stopped for burgers, talk died. He asked me about my week at the beach, but what could I say? *I'm in love with my best friend, whom you don't like because he's Asian and I talk about him too much instead of some girl, and he spent the week ignoring me so I took out my frustrations by stealing a couple of hundred bucks in quarters from all the video games at the hotel where we were staying? Would you mind getting in a wreck and getting this over with for all of us? Pretty please?* Janelle kept her mouth shut. She was probably enjoying this. She was probably on something. She was usually on something.

We reached Belhaven; we parked in a long-term spot; we made our way to the town's modest marina. The Marine's neighbor Gary Mack was his usual charming self, already at least a six-pack into his cooler of beer, stumbling aft to piss into the sound from the side of the boat. He didn't hide his distaste for me and the feeling was mutual. There were one or two others. Once we'd put in the obligatory we're-here-let's-socialize time, Janelle and I slipped away to walk around Belhaven's small, historic downtown.

As soon as we left the marina, I relaxed a little. Being slightly claustrophobic, I couldn't breathe on that boat. I wanted to walk among people without standing out, without being the subject of their conversations. Although I didn't have money to eat in the nice waterfront restaurants or to shop in the boutiques, I wanted to be near these things. Like many towns on the mainland coast, Belhaven oozed quaintness and charm but hadn't been discovered by the Northeast Corridor yet. We window-shopped. We ducked into a secondhand bookstore, and I found a copy of Anne Rice's *Interview with the Vampire*, a book I'd been meaning to read for a couple of years. The Sting song "Moon over Bourbon Street" had finally prompted me to look for it.

"Let's get out of here," I said, book in hand.

"What?" Janelle asked. "You mean, go back to the *boat* now?"

"Fuck no. Let's stay away as long as we can. Don't unpack. Tonight, when everybody's asleep, we're going to take the car and drive back to Greenville. I've already got the keys…"

"Are you *serious*?"

"Let's find a payphone and call Mom collect, to tell her what's going on."

We did. She was horrified. The depression had abated when we left the boat, but the call reminded me why it was there in the first place. I told her how vile Gary Mack was acting, how cramped the boat was, how there was no bathroom to speak of. I had IBS and wasn't sure what was going to happen when I needed to go. What was I supposed to do, take a dump over the side with everyone watching? I didn't tell her that sooner or later someone was going to call me prissy or delicate. Someone was going to scoff at me for not wanting to get dirty; someone was going to criticize my lack of coordination and physical strength. I couldn't stick around for their contempt. I'd long since had enough of being treated like a failed male, and after that depressing week at the beach, I was losing my mind. All those athletic-equipment birthday presents and athletic camps and years on swim teams still hadn't managed to turn me into the sort of son the Marine wanted, he was still trying, and I was frantic to leave before things got any uglier and more painful than they already were. But there was no way I could tell the

Marine any of this. I think Janelle kind of got it, albeit through a haze of pot and hallucinogens.

After hanging up, we walked around, but Belhaven's microscopic downtown didn't offer much distraction and we'd already seen every inch. We—Laura, Janelle, and I—agreed I'd try talking to the Marine before slipping away in the night. He deserved at least that much consideration. Laura wanted us to get out of there as soon as possible, to keep us off the roads late at night. I wasn't worried about that part (what 16-year-old is ever worried about that part?) and I knew the way well enough that getting lost wouldn't be a problem. There was something glamorous about driving fast after midnight. But none of this mattered. One way or another, we were leaving.

Back on the boat, that's exactly what I told the Marine. I felt awful, seeing the look on his face. To his credit, he took the high road and said we could leave. Sweet relief. I'd have grabbed my bag and sprinted for the car right then, but he wanted to Have a Meaningful Father-Son Conversation after giving us his blessing to depart. It was obvious this had hurt him, but it couldn't be helped. He asked increasingly agonized questions, none of which I could answer: What was wrong with me? What had he done? How had things gotten so awkward between us? Why had I shut down like this? The more he asked, the more I withdrew. Saying what I really thought had gotten me the belt too many times in the past. If I'd actually said something along the lines of "If you terrorize your kids pretty much all their lives, they're not going to want to hang out with you later," it would have been... well, Katy bar the door. And the thing with Steve: I understood what it all meant but couldn't even admit it to *myself* yet, much less the Marine.

When it was clear that I couldn't offer much more than

teenage mumbles, the Marine gave up and said, "Well, I'm going to go take a good and healthy crap. Don't leave until I get back, okay?" He ambled off to the marina's restroom.

"Get your stuff," I said to Janelle, who'd been waiting below deck the whole time. "He's gone to take a shit or something, and then we can go."

After about ten minutes, he returned, gave us hugs, and told us to drive safely. I'm pretty sure I didn't do much more than 75 on the highway back to Greenville, maybe 80.

CHAPTER 18: THE NEW REGIME

After the beach trip and the aborted sailing trip (a storm hit the coast that weekend and cut the trip short; we were lucky to leave when we did), I went into free-fall, even if there was no one around to notice. The Marine surprised me with a car for my 16th birthday. A cool one, too: a recently restored 1970 VW Beetle. Forest green, four-speed manual transmission. Black interior, no air conditioning, which meant sweaty drives in the summer and foggy windows when it rained, but... a car! At the very least, it meant I could come and go when I needed to. Being generally unhireable (in places like Greenville, looking like I'd just failed an audition for a Depeche Mode video pretty much ruled out retail and restaurant jobs) and therefore usually too broke to spend much on gas, I tended to stay in my room and read all day. Janelle stayed in her room and bumped all day.

One night toward the end of that terrible summer, we went out for dinner at Villa Roma, an Italian place not too far from home. A Greenville institution, it had been around for years; the swim team would go for pizza and pitchers of Pepsi if we did well in regional meets. It was the kind of dimly lit restaurant with faux-cobbled floors and candle-holders made from empty Chianti bottles wrapped in rattan: cheesy, but it made up for it by serving very good food. I don't know how much Laura had

had to drink before we left the house, how many pills she'd taken. Having just gotten the car, I did the driving. Mercifully, there were no dramatic pronouncements this time about the car being a big box with all our lives in it.

"The ceiling fan's blowing right in my face!" she exclaimed toward the end of the meal. "I can't take it anymore!"

She stood up on tiptoe, reached up, tried to adjust the fan, lost her balance, and pitched to one side. Two waiters rushed over; one caught her before she crashed to the floor and took our table down with her. Everyone in the restaurant stopped eating to watch the commotion. Thirty years later, I can still feel that breathless, heavy pause in the air.

"I want to turn the ceiling fan off!"

Janelle and I looked at each other, all appetite gone. Around us, people started eating again. Conversation resumed, but with a judgmental hush this time.

"Can you drive her home?" one of the waiters asked me.

"I drove us here."

"Good."

As if suddenly realizing she'd just made a scene, Laura settled back into her seat, kind of folded in on herself, and finished her meal. Janelle and I picked at our food.

There were no other tipsy restaurant nights, although she bought a new jug of Taylor Lake Country White every time she bought groceries and either careened around the house at night or retreated into her office. Now and then we'd rent movies (in a rare moment of extravagance, she'd bought a VHS player for the TV), but she was just as likely to stay in her bedroom reading. Years earlier, she'd enrolled as an undergraduate at ECU in order to finish her degree, and was doing it one or two classes at a time. Sometimes she had homework. Being morbid, she also liked revising and updating her will. After all, as she had told us more than once, if she were to be diagnosed with anything fatal, she believed it was essential to have her affairs in order already so that she could go on and kill herself and get it over with. The last thing she wanted was to be a burden.

Some afternoons, she would come home from work and tell us how she had broken down sobbing in the ladies' room. A couple of the housekeeping staff, especially a woman her own age named Rosie, would often follow her in and let her cry on their shoulders. (As far as I know, her white colleagues offered no such support.) After changing clothes and downing a glass or sixteen of wine, she would then throw together a desultory supper and we'd eat, talking very little.

Books got me through the remains of that summer. *Interview with the Vampire* blew off the top of my head when I read it. Homoerotic vampires in New Orleans! With none of the Jeebus silliness! It was like the book I had been waiting my whole life to discover, and the day I finished it, I sped over to the library (the VW was surprisingly fast) to see if I could find its sequel, *The Vampire Lestat*. It was there, as was Rice's standalone novel *Cry to Heaven*, which I also checked out. I loved them both but was back in the abyss after finishing. Somehow one endless day gave way to the next; one endless week turned into another. Now and then there would be a letter or a phone call. What kept me going was the same thing that always had: my weirdly self-contradictory stamina that allowed me to endure the unendurable in hopes that a future I didn't quite believe in might actually surpass expectations and not suck.

Back at S&M that fall, everything felt different. For one thing, I'd switched dorms: I would be rooming with Dan Ingram in 3rd Bryan. Paul and I had fallen out or just grown sick of each other. The idea of rooming together as seniors never came up; we tacitly understood that at the end of junior year, we were done. Dan, a lanky, tie-dye-wearing hippie-genius from Chapel Hill, was one of the more unlikely people I could have ended up with… which was why I asked him in the first place. He was mellow enough that we wouldn't get on each other's nerves (much), we sort of *got* each other, and he had no fucks to give about my sexual orientation and the rumors about it. And the idea of spending another year in Wyche, with its grotty bathrooms and hissing radiators, did not appeal to me at all. Never mind the cockroaches, the place smelled like armpits and ass. Bryan, the dorm that had started out as the patient wing, offered more space and a bathroom in each room. Big windows, too. Lots of sunlight. You had to go down the hall to take a shower, but at least you had your own toilet and sink. I liked some of the guys on the hall (Palmer had moved too, and for the same reasons I had), and several of the new juniors seemed pretty cool. Jason Sullivan from Greenville lived next door, and I hit it off right away with Jim Kim and Tim Clark, who were roommates. It wasn't nirvana, though: a couple of guys openly disliked me, including one of the gay ones who was known to be dating a guy from the class of '86. Typical. I especially loathed Palmer's snide, jeering roommate, Kevin Kirby, the only person at S&M who wasn't from Greenville but might as well have been. From time to time I wondered if I could get away with putting saltpeter in his water bottle so that he wouldn't be able to get hard and bang his girlfriend. No comment on whether I ever actually did it, though, or tried.

A change in administration was behind some of the new chill in the air. A new dean of students, a woman named Patricia Thompson became NCSSM's own real-life Dolores Umbridge some 17 years before she showed up to terrorize Hogwarts in *Harry Potter and the Order of the Phoenix*. A smiling, peroxide-blonde Southern harpy who acted as if she resented us before starting work at S&M (questions were asked, usually in private, about her two sons' suitability for admission), she wasted no time scorching the earth by implementing a draconian new penal code. This included a three-tier demerit system and an all-encompassing set of rules (which she expanded throughout that first semester every time a student did something she hadn't thought of in advance but still wanted to punish them for). Severe penalties for absenteeism, expulsion for low grades, you name it. You'd get back from class and find a form—photocopied, half the size of a sheet of 8½ x 11 paper—under your dorm-room door to inform you you'd been given a Level 1 for this minor infraction or a Level 2 for that one. There were no Kafka-esque quill pens that would magically carve our punishment lines into the backs of our hands, but there might as well have been. A climate of—not fear, exactly, but more like intense, sustained anxiety—had always pervaded at NCSSM. As you'd expect, such a concentration of academically gifted teenagers in one place were always going to come encumbered with baggage and messiness. There were hormones and intelligent rebellions. Patsy Umbridge's new clampdown did nothing to dissuade us from the things we were determined to do, although I seem to recall wallpapering your door with a decoupage of your Level 1 slips itself became a Level 1 infraction.

That semester, I was the first student to have two unexcused absences, and under the new regime, this meant mandatory sessions at the counseling center. One of the new counselors, Bonnie Weathers, an immense black woman who should have been behind a pulpit and not a counselor's desk, took me to task when I told her I'd had diarrhea the second time and hadn't felt like announcing it to the world. This was actually true. Having IBS means sometimes my guts determine where I can and can't go, and when.

"No! When Bonnie have diarrhea, I take some medicine and I go! It's no excuse!"

"Isn't the point of taking diarrhea medicine *not* having to go?"

This did not endear me to her. Worse, she insisted I come back for more sessions.

I made a note to myself: the next time my digestive system was fucked up, consult with Maria Stefansdottir, the sympathetic and rather glamorous school nurse. She seemed to like me. I doubted she'd give me a hard time about this kind of thing, even if what I really needed was the occasional mental-health day. I sensed Maria belonged to a low-key syndicate of teachers and administrators who didn't buy into the new totalitarianism but couldn't openly speak out against it. Several, including Marco Pellegrino, the 3rd Bryan RA, sometimes hinted that they thought the new administration had gone too far, restricting this, banning that, and punishments for everything. Back then, I was just beginning to develop a radar for this sort of thing. Although I had the usual dysfunctional-family refugee's hyperawareness to the moods of the people around me, the anaesthetic fog bank I tended to disappear into blocked out any benefit this vigilance might have offered.

Less interested in getting to know me than in hearing herself talk, Bonnie ranted about the evils of cutting class, about the opportunity that had been given to me, and I let her go on like this, grunting at times in order to simulate attentiveness. It was a skill I'd already perfected with Laura. Besides, it seemed

170

prudent not to challenge her. She'd built up such momentum that resistance would have been like trying to stop a tank barehanded. I couldn't stand her.

As if it weren't enough that S&M's student guidebook now resembled a medieval penal code, the curriculum had been overhauled as well, and my fairly useless academic advisor (I once overheard someone from another department refer to her as "that little dog dyke") had goaded me into registering for classes I didn't want to take. Burnt out on math, quite a bit of which I could already do in my head anyway, I tried to sign up for the senior-level course below the newly combined Calculus 1 and 2. But at the end of junior year, I was too wrecked from everything going on at home (and in my own head) to push back. More to the point, I didn't want to be *challenged*. I wanted to survive another year and get out with my grades more or less intact, but the little dog dyke insisted.

One day, the calculus teacher (she was neither my advisor nor the source of her nickname), kept me after class to talk about a test I'd gotten a 50 on. I am pretty sure she knew something was going on with me (everyone did), and in hindsight I'm not sure that meeting was really about my test score.

"You can remember this much?" she asked. "I know you aren't studying. You can do this just from sitting in class and paying attention? You retain it?"

I nodded, and she looked at me for a moment.

"Not many students could do that. Not at the pace we're going. This isn't easy stuff."

She extracted promises to apply myself, to come to her for help, and I might even have sort of meant them at the time. After that, I did try. I did. I mustered a brief burst of energy and tried to catch up on the calculus I'd blown off (it was already too late, and I think she knew that). Study nights in the library. Reading everything I was assigned, sometimes twice. The reality was, I was drowning. College applications were coming thick and fast in the mail, and the Marine and Laura were too busy arguing to help, and with Sarah Lund (the counselor I'd seen throughout the second half of junior year, who took me to see the movie 9½ Weeks with her two sons in order to cheer me up) gone, only Tom McMillan in the guidance office seemed like someone I'd want to talk to about plans after graduation or anything else. He emanated calm, which made me want to talk to him, but he was gay and therefore I was terrified of him (even if I also thought, and let's be honest, he was quite handsome in a DILF kind of way). I needed to make plans and decisions, but the Marine still viewed himself as my commanding officer, and on the occasions when I couldn't avoid talking to him, he issued commands. Moistly shambolic, Laura got misty whenever the subject of college came up. She'd moan something about having carried me in a special place under her heart for nine months and wander off to the kitchen to refill her wine glass.

I wouldn't say I was suicidal, but I believed in the future about as much as I believed in telekinesis or Jesus. I literally could not envision myself alive and healthy and laughing with friends after class at some university, dating, graduating, moving forward into a life of my own. None of it. Trapped and suffocating, I didn't give a damn about consequences because nothing existed much beyond that hellish *now*. If I'd known then what I do now, I'd have still applied to Brown and Cornell, plus Oberlin, Tulane, and a few of the UNC schools in the distant western half of the state. As it was, I filled out half of my application to Carolina and just gave up.

In fairness, I had fun too. I sought it out because I was tired of being trapped by my circumstances. With Steve out of the picture (I barely heard from him after the beach trip, and once the semester started, not at all) and no more weekends *chez* Zung, I now had to navigate life on campus again. As the weeks went by, I became better friends with my juniors than with many people in my own class. In general, the Class of '88 had a certain spark that my '87 cohort lacked—a coherence, perhaps. And there were 300 of them compared to less than 200 of us. More people on campus, more potential friends. In some ways, life continued on much as it had the year before: talking until late night with Dan and other guys on the hall, sneaking into each other's rooms after curfew, studying until the wee hours, discreetly drinking or smoking weed when we could get our hands on any, making meals out popcorn and ramen noodles on days when the cafeteria food was too nasty to eat. One time, we even made peanut brittle in the chemistry lab, and I ate all of it for dinner to avoid the mystery cutlets and the sour milk. (That fall, the cafeteria lost its grade-A sanitation rating. At the entrance, the certificate bearing a big green C put quite a few of us off our food for a few weeks. The extra pounds everyone had put on from eating cafeteria slop fell away again.)

I even resumed swimming, although it had been a year and my strokes had devolved into a sort of sustained, directional semi-drowning. S&M's swim team had been disbanded before the start of my junior year, and although I had some reservations, I felt like I needed to be back in the water. Enough incoming juniors wanted it reinstated that the administration gave in. I joined, and it felt great apart from the fact that I'd lost what little strength I had and was too tired and hungry all the time to be any good. I'd always had the physique of a box of chopsticks. Now when I tried to do backstroke, my ass kept sinking, and butterfly was even worse: I couldn't manage a single length of the pool. Worse, one of my teammates had a distracting, ginormous horse dick. When he dove in, the thing hit the water five seconds before the rest of him did. Bad enough that I had once sliced through the water and now splashed and flailed and finished gasping for breath like an asthmatic; in the locker room, it was hard not to see physical proof that I was a gangly, out-of-shape assemblage of shortcomings. Meets were exercises in humiliation and I lost events I used to win, but being rather good at annoying perseverance, I pressed on anyway. As the months went by, I became... slightly less bad.

For a moment there, just a moment, I had a glimmer of optimism. I was studying. I could finish my Carolina application and maybe fill out a few others. Fuck Laura and the Marine and their drama. I was swimming again, or trying. I had some old friends and some new ones. Some version of the future might actually happen. I didn't know what it would look like, only that it would be mine.

And then I set the school on fire.

CHAPTER 19: PYROKINESIS

A couple of months into the semester, a Friday night went badly. Two juniors and I went over to Duke to see if we could find a party to crash, a time-honored NCSSM tradition for students who wanted to get drunk. We succeeded. That part wasn't difficult. I knew someone there, and although we didn't find him, we did find a party. Besides, dorms weren't locked back in the '80s because there was no risk of a lunatic with a Kalashnikov bursting in and shooting the place up. You could walk right in, wander the halls until you found an open door, music, and a keg, and invite yourself in. I always radiated Nervous Dork Energy, which I think got us pegged as marauding S&Mers on one or two previous party raids. This time, things got a little complicated when Irina, whom I knew from the swim team, chugged a can of Coke that was (oops) mostly vodka.

Myself, I wasn't drinking that night. Which is to say, I might have had one little plastic cup of beer. I had a swim meet in the morning and needed my sleep if I was to have any hope of keeping pool water out of my lungs and reaching the finish line. And Chris, the other student with us, was diabetic, so he might have had a sip or two, nothing more. In addition to the toxic can of Coke, Irina may have had a couple of beers. The alcohol hit her almost instantly and within minutes she was stumbling drunk.

"Did she eat dinner?" one of the Duke students asked.

I looked at Chris. He shook his head.

Irina tried to stand up. Her legs gave way, she collapsed back into her chair, she slumped over to one side, eyes fluttering, face slack, and I knew we were probably fucked.

"We need to get her back to her room, and we're going to need at least one girl to help," I said. "And her roommate. Who can we trust?"

Chris and I hauled Irina to her feet and helped her out the door. The night was colder than I'd dressed for. North Carolina can be like that: the beautiful lingering warmth of early fall departs in a snap when the sun sets, and that crispness takes on a sharp edge, especially in the central and western parts of the state. We stumbled out into the night, trying to remember our way across the darkly Gothic campus and back to 9th Street. That's the thing with Duke: though it's stunning by day, the campus looks like the set of a horror movie if you're in trouble after sunset. We made it as far as Erwin Road, which changes name and becomes 9th Street when it crosses underneath the Durham Freeway. There was some road work going on, and we draped a semiconscious Irina across an orange barrel topped with a blinking yellow light while we rested.

A black Mercedes came to a stop beside us. The driver rolled down his window and leaned out.

"Your friend's pretty drunk. Do you guys need a ride?"

Duke students to the rescue. We managed to hoist Irina into the back seat between us. She came to long enough to start babbling "I want to give you a blowjob! I want to give you a blowjob!", so I stuck my finger in her mouth to shut her up. It was perhaps not the wisest choice I made that night, but at

176

least she managed not to start vomiting until she was back in her room.

Her RA drove her to Duke Hospital. Irina ended up needing to have her stomach pumped, and they gave her activated charcoal. And Chris and I were kept up all night being questioned about our roles in the affair: How much had she drunk? Had we had any alcohol ourselves? Why had we gone to Duke looking for a party if we hadn't intended to drink? Why as a senior had I not shown better leadership? And so on. Guilty until proven innocent.

With less than two hours' sleep and no breakfast, I did as dismal a job in the water the next morning as could be expected.

All three of us were suspended for a couple of days (it meant a long weekend at home), then brought back on academic probation. And, as is often the case with me after something acutely stressful, I came down with some kind of cold/flu bug. After three or four days in bed with a cough and a fountaining nose, dutifully excused from class each day by Maria, I got sick and tired of smelling sick and tired. Even after I showered, the lingering scent of armpits and sputum in the room grossed me out. Dan was too polite to complain, but I noticed him noticing it. Since the weather had turned too chilly to leave the windows open for long, I lit a scented votive candle and set it on the glass shelf above the sink.

Growing up, I did this all the time. The Marine and Laura may have scoffed at the '60s but they were products of their times: candles, potted plants, wicker baskets everywhere. After Vietnam, the Marine hated incense and pretty much anything else even remotely suggestive of Asia, but with him gone, I liked the sweet fog of it. And it covered up the smell of pot smoke quite effectively.

That afternoon, about four days into the cold, thoroughly sick of blowing snot-torrents into boxes of Kleenex, I was in a vile mood. My nose and upper lip were chafed. Everything hurt. Standing in front of the sink, I blew my nose for the ten-thousandth time, stared into the candle that burned on the ledge over the sink. I then rolled the snotty tissue into a cylinder and stuck one end into the flame, held it there just long enough to make sure the dry end of the paper had caught, and stepped back. I let it burn for a second. The fire advanced slowly, slowed down by the snot.

"Burn, you fucker."

I turned on the water and doused the burning tissue-roll. Once (I thought) the fire was out, I tossed it in the (cardboard box full of paper) trash beneath the sink. I turned away and took a single step. A low sound made me turn back: FWUMP! Tiny flames flickered amid the tissues and paper towels.

This time, there was no hand-wringing "oh my God" moment of disbelief. I understood what had happened, understood what it meant. When I stepped back to the sink and tried to stomp out the flames (perhaps also not my wisest choice ever, even if I was foggy from antihistamines), the action of my foot plunging into the garbage box sent burning bits of paper into the air. Some landed on the carpet. My pants didn't catch fire, fortunately, but the carpet did. When the stomping didn't work, I tried water. The largest vessel at hand was the Corningware bowl Dan used for ramen noodles. I filled this at the sink and tossed it into the burning trash, then repeated the procedure. However, the trash was now crackling like a campfire and the carpet had caught. Nothing in the room would work fast enough, so I dashed down the hall to get a fire extinguisher.

The thing wouldn't come out of its metal brackets. I tried

lifting, twisting, unfastening... nothing worked.

Meanwhile, my fucking *room* was burning.

If there had ever been a moment for an adrenaline rush, this was it. Desperate, I jerked the entire assemblage out of the plaster and raced back down the hall. Mercifully, the fire extinguisher itself was easy to use. I pointed it at the fire and pulled the trigger.

A thick stream of white shit shot out of it. "Oh *fuck*." I'd been expecting... water? Foam? Not a deluge of dense semi-liquid white powder. Somewhere in the back of my head, I was thinking *this is going to be hard to clean up, later*, but that was of less importance than putting out the goddamn fire. When I was convinced I'd done that, I slipped back into planning mode.

That afternoon was the start of an extended weekend, which meant Laura and—even better—Janelle were on the way to Durham to pick me up. (We weren't allowed to have cars on campus or I'd have driven myself home.) For once, I was profoundly glad they were coming.

With the fire now out except for some residual smoke drifting up from the scorched patches of carpet, I set the fire extinguisher down.

There was one more detail to take care of, before I slipped outside to join the evacuation. Moving fast, I unzipped my beanbag chair, reached inside, and fished around for the plastic baggie containing a smaller bag of pot and my pipe. I rolled this into the smallest, tightest package possible and stuck it in my right pocket. I zipped the beanbag shut again, careful to pick up the few tufts of foam that had burst out of it, lest anyone notice and ask questions. I then set the fire extinguisher just inside the door, which I locked behind myself when I stepped out into the hall.

Around me, fire alarms were blaring; students were evacuating in a semi-orderly fashion. The ones who'd had boring classes would probably thank me for this later, I thought vaguely. Did I really think I was going to get away with it? No, I didn't. From this vantage point some decades years later, I can honestly say it wouldn't have occurred to me to go anyone in the administration to say I'd done this by accident. Not with Madame Martinet in charge. Not only had the whole tone of things at S&M changed from the previous year—institutional and impersonal where before it had felt more like a group of people who could at least sort of relate to each other—but after my suspension, I was on thin ice and I knew it.

I waited outside with everybody else.

Someone came up to me: "Hey Marshall, your room's on fire!"

"Oh shit! Are you sure?" Okay, I know it was stupid. I casually looked down to see if my pants were smudged with fire extinguisher splooge. They were not.

When everyone was allowed back in, I was intercepted by Kirk Curtis, the head of security, and by Dennis Williams, now the head RA. They wouldn't let me into my room. They'd need to ask me questions. Dan had been in class, so there was no question about *who* had done this, just *how*.

"Thank God my plants are okay," I said, surveying the damage.

Kirk blanched. He spluttered, "Your *plants*?"

"Obviously nobody got hurt," I said. "So there's no need to worry about the people. I put the fire out…"

"No you didn't," he said.

The snowball rolling downhill turned into an avalanche.

"Would I have gone outside and left my room *burning*?"

"I don't know. Would you have? Did you?" You could have wrung pure disgust—my favorite emotion!—from his voice like water from a washcloth.

Petrified they would think to search my pockets, I decided not to take any chances.

"I'm getting a headache. Do you guys mind if I go take some aspirin?" Kirk and Dennis both looked at me like I was nuts. "I have the flu, remember?"

Dennis made me open the bottle. I held it out. He looked inside. I jiggled the pills.

"Aspirin," I said.

I didn't have a headache at all. I wanted to duck into one of the bathrooms down the hall and stick the bag of weed in my sock. It seemed safer. I figured it wouldn't fall out and was less likely to be noticed there. With that out of the way, I popped a couple of Excedrin as a preventive measure (I knew myself well enough; it was only a matter of time before I really would have a raging headache) and trudged back to my room, where smug Oliver Norton was taking pictures of the damage.

Dan was remarkably calm about the whole thing. He just said, "You're cleaning this up. Good luck. See you Tuesday night," and left.

Laura and Janelle arrived: perfect timing.

Both were horrified. I explained it was an accident. I am many things, but I am not an arsonist and never have been.

In a brief moment alone in the room with Janelle, I told her to open her purse.

"What?"

"Just do it." When she did, I bent down, fished the dope out of my sock, and put it in her purse. "Get rid of this. Don't let anyone suspect."

Her eyes lit up. I figured she'd smoke some of it and eventually I'd get the pipe back from her—maybe some of the weed—in Greenville. I already knew she had a one-hitter for those long dull days at Rose High. She told me she sometimes got high in class. She and a couple of other baby hellraisers sat in the back of the room, next to windows they could open. When things got dull and the teacher's back was turned, they'd take a hit or two to add some sparkle to their day.

The glow of relief from concealing the pot got me through the rest of that afternoon. There was a meeting with Patricia Umbridge, but she didn't have much to say: they'd be conducting an investigation, but I should return to school on Tuesday, as scheduled. Having expected to be expelled on the spot, I felt the first itchy stirrings of hope.

"This looks bad," Laura said, driving home. We stopped somewhere for burgers, then got back on the road.

I just wanted to get home, so Janelle and I could sneak out and get fucked up. I did not particularly want to be having this conversation.

"It was an accident!" I protested.

Back then, I still thought that if you tell the truth, people will believe you. That wasn't how things worked out, though.

CHAPTER 20: KAFKA WOULD HAVE ROLLED HIS EYES

A letter came in the mail, addressed to Laura, return address NCSSM. My guts gave a lurch. I wanted to read it but wasn't sure I should. I was in enough hot water already. When she finished reading, she handed it to me and looked at me in disbelief.

"They're... pressing charges?" she asked, clearly unable to get her head around the idea, handing me the tri-folded slip of paper.

I had to read the list a couple of times before the full lunatic weight of it really hit me, a screaming wallop of the bad and the absurd:

- Arson
- Theft of state property
- Destruction of state property
- Endangerment of a minor (multiple counts, and two separate cases—not just the fire but the night at Duke with Irina and Chris)
- Juvenile delinquency (multiple counts)
- Contributing to the delinquency of a minor
- Possession of illegal drugs
- Consumption of illegal drugs

- Possession of alcohol
- Consumption of alcohol

There were probably more, but it's been a few decades. The point was clear: someone in the administration wanted me gone, whatever it took.

"It was a fucking *accident!*" I spluttered.

The parts about drugs and alcohol confused me. As far as I can recall, I never had alcohol on campus that semester. Oh, I drank now and then—we all did—but only when somebody else procured it. As for the weed, well, yes, that part was true, but I'd gotten rid of it and they had no proof other than Irina's word against mine.

For perhaps the first time since my days on the swim team, the Marine and Laura emerged from their respective miasmas of pills, booze, and mutual loathing, and turned out to be... surprisingly effective. The Marine hired a lawyer, a crisp blonde woman who met with me once and told me not to lie.

"I can only help you if I know the full truth. I'm not here to judge you, to tell your parents, or to get you in trouble. But I can only get you out of trouble if you tell me exactly what you did and didn't do."

So I did, and within a couple of days' time, she got back to us with good news: the administration had backed down. They couldn't pursue a criminal case. They'd have been laughed out of court. They didn't have any evidence, only hearsay from a student who'd gotten drunk and whom I'd helped get back to campus. They couldn't prove *intent*. The attorney also now had an explanation for two of the more baffling charges, theft and destruction of state property: these stemmed from me pulling the fire extinguisher and its holder out of the wall, then leaving it in my room and locking the door afterward.

"How the fuck was that theft?" I asked. "That's just... cleaning up after yourself."

"These people are idiots," Laura said.

There turned out to be no structural damage to the room itself, not even scorch marks on the tile floor. Since the carpet belonged to me—it was a leftover piece from the King George house—and the furniture could be cleaned, and since I'd immediately attempted to put the fire out, none of these charges would stand up in court. As for the bit about drugs and alcohol, had I *given* Irina drugs and alcohol? I had not. She helped herself to booze at a party at Duke, and I had no way of knowing she'd get sick. Had she ever seen this bag of pot I supposedly had, or smoked any? She had not. At best, the administration could charge me with a succession of stupid decisions, but nothing criminal.

There was still going to be an expulsion hearing, however. The attorney couldn't make *that* go away.

I was allowed to return to campus and resume my classes, but forbidden to talk to Irina. Of course we got together and talked anyway. I was sort of angry at her and sort of not: she was under pressure and trying to save her own ass. I got it. Her parents seemed to believe I had poured booze down her throat with rape in mind (for once, being the Big Fag on Campus should have been useful but wasn't) and the administration seemed to believe I was the Antichrist. From the moment I got back to S&M, I found myself at the eye of a storm of whispers and sideways glances. Mostly I ignored them. Of course people were talking, but after a lifetime as the subject of gossip, it was hard to care much. In general, the students and even the teachers seemed sympathetic: the fire had been an accident, everyone knew that, we'd put it out, no one had been hurt, so why couldn't we just move on?

The afternoon of the hearing: Laura and I met with Dr. Callahan, my academic advisor that year, who had never advised me about anything that I can recall. He taught physics. Clearly at a loss for words, or at least helpful ones, he spun a long incomprehensible story about the beginning of his career as an engineer. He'd been hired to design a wooden bridge in some remote logging corner of Canada. Possibly Maine. Some cold place with big trees. Having taken the necessary measurements—how far apart the banks of the river were, how high the span would have to be, and so on—and calculated the necessary tolerances, he then went overboard. He didn't need to design an indestructible bridge, just a serviceable one, but he was fresh out of grad school and keen to impress his employers. This überbridge required the loggers to scour the forest for the largest tree…

I noticed Laura's eyes drooping. She'd just made the drive up from Greenville and was probably on something. Dr. Callahan was putting us both to sleep. I gave a moment's silent thanks never to have taken any of his classes. The consensus among his students was that he was nice enough, but good luck staying awake.

At the point in the story when the Big Bad Wolf should have livened things up by leaping from behind a mighty oak and devouring the stalwart loggers, both the plot and Dr. Callahan's voice gave out. There wasn't much of an ending. They found the tree. They built the bridge. Much later, he looked back and realized his mistake. He could have designed a smaller and less ambitious bridge. Less time and effort would have gone into the construction. His employers would have been even *more* impressed. I searched for a way to connect this parable to my imminent expulsion. Hope fuels optimism, but they're not the same thing. Maybe he was just trying to pass the time, not knowing what else to say.

"I just try to keep my head above water," Dr. Callahan said, seemingly in conclusion. "It's best not to stick it up too high, but it's not a good idea to go under, either." He punctuated this with a dry little chuckle. I looked at the strands of his comb-over. It was almost time to go downstairs. "Then you drown!"

We said our goodbyes, and he wished me luck.

"He's an idiot," Laura said as we walked down the hall. "When he was talking about keeping his head above water, you know what I thought of? I just wanted to say, *Like a turd in the tide?*"

I giggled a little but my humor faded fast in the conference room.

It wasn't a hearing, it was a banana-republic show trial with a preordained outcome.

Donna, the 2nd Bryan RA: I didn't respect the rules. A few weeks earlier, when I got caught violating curfew, and had friends in my room after 11.00, I broke into really forced-sounding laughter at the prospect of getting a Level 1 demerit.

Kirk, the head of security: I had obviously been burning something in my sink. Dan and I were both menaces to the school, as evidenced by the fact that Dan had burnt a demerit slip a couple of weeks earlier, placed it in a baggie, and posted it on our door. (Kirk seemed to miss the distinction that Dan and I were not the same person.) He, Kirk, didn't believe my account of what happened. In his estimation, I had been burning something in the sink, and the fire had leapt from the sink to the box of trash beneath the sink.

At this point, if the outcome hadn't already been obvious,

it was now. God forbid someone at the fucking North Carolina School of Science and Mathematics should have pointed out that there's this thing called physics and fire doesn't jump out of sinks and into trash cans below. However, the only teacher in the room was gay and terrifying (he would later be arrested on charges of kidnapping, assault, and crimes against nature— he allegedly abducted a 20-year-old guy with nefarious deeds in mind), a lounge lizardy type who taught English and was widely regarded as useless.

Kirk went on: I was obviously doing something malicious and destructive, and it was equally obvious that I had no concern about my fellow students. After all, I was more worried about my plants. He quoted my comment from the day of the fire as if he'd never heard anything more psychopathic in his life.

This was the moment in my life when I learned I don't do emotional command performances. If you want me to emote at you and I've already processed the situation and moved on, I probably won't, and it makes you uncomfortable, I don't care. So there's that.

I believe Dennis even got in on the action. I had a toaster oven in my room, and those were banned. Didn't I know that?

"Since when?"

Since they had retroactively changed the rules in order to have something else to throw at me, as it turned out, and issued a directive to the RAs to that effect. It wasn't in the student handbook. Half the students had toaster ovens in their rooms. The cafeteria had a C sanitation rating. What else were we supposed to do in order to eat food that wasn't seething with salmonella?

Gay and Terrifying, bored, piped up, wanting to know how I'd started the fire.

"With a lighter?"

"And where did you *get* the cigarette lighter?"

"At a convenience store? Where everyone else buys them?"

"*Which* convenience store?"

"I don't know?"

Someone else was brought in to talk about my awful grades and poor attendance (two unexcused absences plus a few sick days and the suspensions). It was pointed out that if I hadn't gotten in so much trouble, I was in danger of flunking out (because of that fucking calculus class I hadn't wanted to take in the first place).

"What's wrong, Marshall?" asked Patsy Umbridge. "You're one of the brightest students at this school, and your grades have dropped so much..."

It was like being back on the boat in Belhaven all over again, with the Marine asking more or less the same question, demanding that I explain things that were too big for the words I had then. How was I supposed to explain that my grandfather was basically a murderer and had died in jail during my junior year and I wasn't allowed to talk about it? An abusive, alcoholic Vietnam vet with PTSD for a father and an angry, clinging, devastated Southern belle-manque alcoholic for a mother? That my parents were splitting up and it was ugly and my sister was a borderline catatonic with a drug problem and I was stuck in the middle? That I was gay and not really okay with it and had been bullied and beaten up all my life? That I'd fallen in some version of love for the first time and been dumped? And there was no one I could talk to about *any* of it? Any of these items by itself was already too much, and these assholes wanted teenage excuses that would fit into their repertoire of scolding: "I've been drinking." "My parents are splitting up and I'm so

189

sad, I've been acting out." "I can't handle the pressure here anymore." Not, "I know I fucked up but if you kick me out, you're probably sending me back to my death."

We could all see the verdict coming from a mile away, but I remained in denial until Patsy Umbridge read the committee's decision: the school would accept my voluntary withdrawal. If I chose not to withdraw, formal expulsion proceedings would begin. My family and I would have the right to appeal, in the case of expulsion, and we could also pursue legal redress.

In the hall afterward, I was numb with shock.

"If I hadn't known you wanted to stay here so bad..." the Marine started to say. He hesitated, an even longer pause than usual for him. "Let me put it this way. That hearing was a crock of shit. About halfway through, I wanted to lean forward and tell you to tell them to shove this school as far up their asses as it would go."

The Marine's anger partly vanished after the hearing and partly didn't. Within a few days he went back to doing what he always did, redirecting it toward me. With only two or three weeks left of the semester, the administrators threw me a bone and decided I could finish my courses. It didn't occur to me to ask why. I was over the edge of the world, shell-shocked out of my goddamn mind. Between themselves, the Marine and Laura decided that the Friday after the hearing, he would borrow a truck, drive up to Durham, pick up me and most of my stuff; we'd leave behind just enough clothes and personal items for those final weeks. I would then drive back to campus myself on the following Sunday. The assholes had already kicked me out. If they didn't like me having a car on campus, what were they going to do? Kick me out again?

He arrived before I was done packing, and in a spluttering

rage, started throwing things into boxes. Glasses broke; book pages tore. When I objected, he erupted. So angry his accent thickened and he could hardly pronounce the longer words he was trying to say, he launched into a tirade about how irresponsible I'd been, how great this opportunity had been, how I'd pissed it away, how I was going back to Rose High so fast my head would spin.

I hadn't even considered this. Back to Rose? Everything I'd taken surpassed the most advanced classes offered there. There was literally nothing left I could take. I'd be better off getting a GED and going straight to ECU, but when I tried pointing this out, the words bounced off him. No, I was going back to Rose, he insisted. Only dropouts got GEDs, and he hadn't raised a fucking high school dropout.

I declined to point out that actually, he had. Once we'd finished packing/destroying most of my personal belongings and loading them in the truck, we had to leave. When I tried to say goodbye to a couple of my friends, he barked "Get in the truck!", shocking them. Apart from a couple of *sotto voce* mutterings about how he couldn't believe I had pissed away (he kept using that phrase) my opportunity at S&M, he barely spoke to me on the two-hour trip back. Somehow this was worse than the nonstop lecture I'd been expecting. Hadn't he just three days earlier said the expulsion hearing was full of shit? Had he already forgotten the fire was an accident?

Those final couple of weeks passed in an overcast, wintry blur. The bleakness of the season matched my internal landscape, all grey and black and damp with sadness. It felt good to have the car on campus, a sort of fuck-you to Patsy and Kirk and Dennis and the other assclowns in that meeting. I had a feeling they knew the green Beetle at the edge of the parking lot belonged to me. Kirk and the security staff must have known, at the very least. Nobody said a word, though. I did use it to sneak off campus with Emma Richards one night when the cafeteria food was especially bad. We couldn't identify the mystery cutlet and the dollop of slop on the side, much less eat them, and as usual, the milk smelled like the cow had been dead. I practically crapped on myself when I started the engine, and I made Emma duck out of sight to attract less attention. We made it off campus without sirens blaring and guards being dispatched. There were no helicopters. Illicit burgers and fries have never tasted so good.

I skipped about half of my remaining classes.

"I've got expulsionitis," I said to Maria every day when I stopped at the infirmary.

"Sounds awful," she'd say, adding my name to the list of sick students. "Hope you feel better soon. Let me know if you need anything."

It took years to learn how much my expulsion had saddened and angered people. It took writing this book. My friends were upset, of course. A couple of my teachers told me through clenched teeth that this was unfair. They were shocked and disappointed—but apart from very basic questions about grades and attendance, no one had solicited their opinions. The ones who had had me in class didn't want me to go. Oh, of course there was a contingent—mostly students I didn't hang out with—who saw the case in black and white: I broke the rules, this was the penalty, good riddance. But I've since heard that among the alumni, the Class of '87 is the one that donates the least money to the school. There's less committee work, less engagement. By far. This is less to do with what happened to me than about the way all of us were treated that year, compared to when we were juniors. Even so, I take a certain satisfaction in knowing it.

Those final days were awkward and sad. We didn't have the Internet, and long-distance calls were expensive, so inevitably I wouldn't see some of these people again. Numb, I trudged through my last classes. Finals, I treated as sort of a joke. The only one I remember taking is calculus because I drew pictures on it. After a tentative first few minutes, thinking I might see if there were any mental muscles left to flex, I gave up. The exam didn't matter. This wasn't angst-powered teenage hyperbole: my college arrangements had already been made, more or less. Less than 20 minutes after starting, maybe 10, I got up and turned in the test. The teacher looked annoyed, but I shrugged. A few of my classmates stopped working and looked up at me in a surprise that quickly gave way to comprehension. A couple of them nodded. Before the door shut behind me, I heard everyone in the room get back to work.

PART THREE: ALMA MURDER

CHAPTER 21: THE PERILS OF A LITTLE EDUCATION

So, Greenville again. Driving back from Durham, I was too shocked to take stock. Thoughts rose and sank in my head like the blobs in a lava lamp. Was I coming back to Greenville in disgrace? Was that even the right way of looking at it? Apart from a few assholes at school, nobody seemed to think what had happened to me was fair. I certainly didn't think so. Maybe it wasn't even about me, not completely: the administration wanted to make an example out of somebody and my chain of screw-ups gave them that chance. After all, legend had it that the administration liked to make an example of one student a year in order to keep the rest of us in line. And when you've grown up being beaten at home and jumped on the street, shouted at and called names, spat upon and on one occasion forced by bullies to kneel down and kiss their bike tires, well, it doesn't come as much of a surprise when someone bigger and more powerful decides they want to destroy you. That's just... Tuesday. The Marine was livid and raving but when was he not? It was all too much and too soon for me to have any perspective yet, and on some level I understood this. In the meantime, it was rainy and cold, and the windshield kept fogging up. The VW's rear-window defogger didn't work, and a fuse would blow if I tried turning it on. This also happened if I switched on the windshield wipers while the stereo was on. All I could do was run the heater and crack the windows just enough to let in a trickle of cool air. Now and then I'd wipe the windows with the sleeve of my jacket. Somewhat grateful for the distraction, I crossed the city limits in less despair than would have been the case in better weather. An early night had fallen, the streets were slick, and the blurry lights of the university hospital and medical complex on the west edge of town formed a wet mirage, reminding me of buildings in a much larger city.

It would have been nice to get home to an empty house, but I couldn't avoid arriving around dinnertime. For once, Laura neither made the moment about herself nor told me what my emotions were. After I unpacked the car, we had dinner. She gave me a beer. Not wanting to talk, I went into my room afterward, shut the door, and read. That was pretty much that. Not so many months ago, I'd been home in this new house for the summer, so in a peculiar way, it was as if things were getting back to normal. As if I'd never left. Only I had.

Two good things happened immediately after my return, although I didn't recognize them as such until later. The first was that I finally started standing up to the Marine. He remained adamant that I should go back to Rose, but his reasons made no sense. No longer willing to take "Because I said so" for an answer, I pushed back. After the aborted sailing trip in Belhaven, the boundaries of our relationship were clear enough. Perhaps he even blamed himself for some of what had happened and was lashing out because of how that made him feel. Or perhaps the easiest way to deal with an awkward nerdy son he hadn't managed to beat the sissy tendencies out of was at a distance, and having me back in town added a second layer to his public shame. I've never asked. In those first days, despite being so traumatized that my hands shook most of the time and I could hardly sleep, I pulled myself together and with a certain exhausted resignation decided there was no point trying to convince him of anything further. Rational discussions wouldn't work and for the most part never had. This time, I knew what I was talking about and he didn't. Simple as that. Since he had made up his mind to be useless, I had to outmaneuver him instead.

The second good thing followed from this: my decision to play my parents against each other. I'd never done that before, or not on purpose. Back in the '80s when everybody's parents were getting divorced, the stories were legend. Literally: it's a common plot device in books, TV shows, and movies from that decade. It's a cliché. When I was younger, I thought it was dishonest and kind of slimy. Then I got old enough to see my parents more clearly. Going back to Rose High would have been unendurable. The Marine and Laura were too messed up to look out for me and perhaps always had been, and there was no point in pretending otherwise. If I was going to be stuck back in Greenville—I didn't even want to think about how many years I might have to be there—I would have to start taking matters into my own hands. The Marine didn't want me to get a GED, which made Laura only too happy to arrange it for me. A phone call or two, a couple of forms, and a modest payment (I think the fee was about $25), and it was done.

The first time I saw him after that, he glared at me and said, "You went around me."

"What did you expect? You weren't listening."

Considering his actions later, I think there was another motivation: according to the terms of the separation, he was on the hook for my college tuition, and he didn't want to pay it. If I went back to Rose, it would let him put off that expense until later in the year.

On the morning of my appointment, a couple of weeks later, I drove over to Pitt Community College to take the pre-tests. On the way, I fretted. What if the test was harder than I was expecting? Rationally, I knew this was ridiculous: if I couldn't pass it, having just left NCSSM, then no one could. On the other hand, what if I fucked it up somehow? Disaster seemed to be my new *modus operandi*. Would I be able to take it again? Would Laura change her mind and side with the Marine, forcing me to go back to Rose? Christ, what would *that* be like? My thoughts turned bleaker and bleaker as I came up with one bad outcome after another.

Before I took the pre-test, the women administering it asked if I wanted study time first. I looked around the room: white cinder-block walls, freshly painted; green and orange plastic chairs from the '70s at every wobbly desk; a big clock on one wall about five minutes fast. I could see several other people in their late teens and twenties crouching over books. Anxiety hung in the air. I could sympathize. Their stories were different from mine, but I'd been there.

"No, I'll just do it."

When I sat down to take the pretest, I flipped through the book... and quietly chuckled in relief. If the pretest was any indication, I would finish the whole thing inside of two hours, possibly less if they'd let me. The questions were so basic, I could have passed the test after the sixth or seventh grade. Very simple grammar and math. Science concepts I'd learned at Pace Academy even before it changed names to Carolina Country Day.

That's more or less how it happened, too. According to the regulations, I couldn't take the test the same day as the pre-test, so I had to make an appointment to return for the first two sections of the GED. I finished them so fast the test administrators looked concerned.

"Are you sure you don't need more time?"

"It's easy."

They scored the first section on the spot—math or English; I don't remember.

"Oh my." The woman who'd done the actual scoring summoned her colleague. "Look at this."

"What?" I asked, panicking.

"No one has ever scored this high on it before. Not since I've been here. You ever seen anything like that before?"

They looked up at me.

"You must be real smart," one of them said.

My face got hot and burned off the fog of disaster scenarios in my head.

"Can I just take the next one now, please?"

I roared through it, handed it in. This time both women crowded together to see how I'd score on it.

Same result.

They looked up at me, seemingly at a loss for words.

"Can I go on to the next section?" I asked.

"No, I'm sorry, the rules don't allow it. We have to give each person a two-hour block of time for each section. You'll have to come back..."

So I did, the next day, and flew through the remaining sections as quickly as I'd taken the first, passed with the same high scores. As simple as that — and I do mean it, literally, simple — was done with high school. For the first time, I wondered why I'd gone on to S&M if this had been an option all along. Why did I stick around for the bullying if I could have left after the 10th grade and gone on to college?

Not liking the fact he'd been outmaneuvered, the Marine decided to supervise my enrollment procedures. I would do one quarter at Pitt Community College, he decreed, and after that I'd start at ECU in the second summer session.

"Why can't I just start in the fall?"

"I don't want you to have too much time on your hands and be out there getting in trouble!" he insisted, as if I were a lifelong hoodlum just paroled from reform school.

So, in a case of history not just repeating itself but satirizing itself, he insisted that I take College Algebra I at PCC.

"But I've already taken Calculus 1!" I objected.

He glared at me. Later, it would occur to me that he might not have known the difference. I also registered for a psychology course and something else I don't remember now, and less than two weeks later, I started at PCC.

The only thing of note about that quarter is the weird mix of emotions I felt at the start. Humiliation, for one thing. It was about as far from Princeton or Stanford as you could get; I also wouldn't be going to the Olympics; and despite my growing resentment of my parents' expectations, even I had to admit I'd been capable of more. But then, being completely honest with myself, I was also relieved. The story of my life had always been about a mandate for greatness. When you're an exceptional kid, you go along with it because it's flattering and you get rewarded and so forth. There's a downside, though: it's not very authentic, and there's the risk of being made to feel like a trained seal barking and clapping its flippers for a tasty fish. No matter how well equipped you are between the ears, the stars still have to line up a certain way for the scholarships and cancer cures and Nobel Prizes and Olympic medals to ensue. For some people, survival is the achievement. If all this meant that I could eventually figure things out on my own without being *told* who I was, what I felt, and where my life was going, then... it might not have been the worst possible outcome.

Now that I was back in Greenville, I didn't feel I could rock the Depeche Mode peroxide and earrings like fishing lures. I got my hair cut short and started dressing in more subdued clothes. (According to my friends at S&M, a new fad took hold after I left: people started dyeing their hair black and doing heroin. One guy OD'ed and his friends kept watch over him in his dorm room until he came to. And the administration thought *I* was a menace?) But the rebellion wasn't over: I got my right ear pierced too. Guys didn't do that back then, not if they didn't want to announce "I'm gay!" to the world. Even though I hadn't really come out, and even though I knew perfectly well what that second piercing signified, I did it anyway. In this midst of this calamity, I felt a peculiar pride at being in college already and only sixteen. (Hell, I needed *something* to be proud of.) I'd been the third-youngest in the Class of '87, and at least a quarter of '88 was older than me as well. They were still in the silver-plated penal colony and I'd broken free, albeit by accident. I couldn't reconcile all these conflicting emotions so I just let them pummel me whenever a new one emerged and felt like taking over. Beer helped.

Toward the end of that quarter at PCC, I went over to ECU to attend an early student-orientation talk and get registered. The only thing I remember from orientation was the speaker—a girl, either a junior or a senior—saying Symbolic Logic was the hardest course the university offered. Even though we could take it in lieu of the required math courses, we probably shouldn't. Which is why I registered for it and took it that summer. (I got an A, too, and even managed to ace the final exam while hallucinating on a dose of cold medicine I didn't know I was allergic to. Everything in the classroom was covered with nonexistent green leaves.)

Whereas PCC had felt like an extension of Rose High, ECU felt more like NCSSM: staggered schedules, no bells between classes, more autonomy for the students. During the registration period, I hiked from department to department to see what I could place out of. ECU is a large campus with a lot of red-brick buildings from the 1960s spread far apart, and July in eastern North Carolina is hell's blazing furnace. That algebra course the Marine had insisted I take at PCC had never been necessary, so the math requirement was out of the way (and would have been, anyway). The other two courses transferred straight in, as well, and I placed into Latin 3. I got credit for a couple of undergraduate English courses and placed into the honors program. The upshot of all those placement tests and conversations was that I was effectively a sophomore by fall, at 17. While that part was cool, what interested me more was that I'd made a couple of friends at orientation and promised to reconnect with them when they came back for the start of classes in the fall. Accomplishment, I could handle. Loneliness, not so much.

Everything was off to a bizarrely promising start. I was in college. There were fewer nuisances, too. At any given moment, Laura and Janelle were intoxicated, semiconscious, and therefore less clingy and annoying. I'd fallen back in with some of my old friends (well, acquaintances who had put up with me at the same lunch table before and now seemed to think I was cool because I was a smart fuckup), a couple of whom had older brothers who would buy us booze. I might even have had the first of the long series of shitty part-time jobs I held throughout college. And, truth be told, as bitterly as I missed my friends and as much as I hated being back within the gamma radiation of my ex-nuclear family, I was also relieved to be done with NCSSM.

Naturally, because it wouldn't do for things to go right for more than fifteen minutes at a stretch, it didn't take long before someone decided to kill me.

It wasn't even homophobia, the obvious motivation, the one you can't be gay and Southern without sort of expecting; nor was it one of my parents, drunk and maudlin and convinced we all be better off together as a family forever and ever. It was much simpler than that, a hammered redneck high school dropout with a Camaro and a gun. Carl [name changed to protect the guilty] was either dating my sister or wanted to be. We were at a party at somebody's house and he showed up uninvited, already at least a six-pack in and bellowing good-ol'-boy bullshit. A typical Greenville evening, in other words. Still newly prodigal and scandalous enough to warrant an invite, I was grateful anybody wanted me around. It didn't occur to me then that the interest was less about me (no one cared) than the story. Somehow I thought this would... I don't know, insulate me from people who had never liked me in the first place? Raise my status? Anyway, it didn't matter. Hanging out at a party on a Saturday night watching acquaintances and frenemies from high school get drunk was better than loneliness, better than sitting at home watching Laura do the same thing, and definitely better than talking to Laura while she lay drunk in bed probably very well aware that I could see her lady parts through her sheer nightgowns.

Picture the scene: a bunch of high school students in a cookie-cutter ranch house built in the late '60s. Three bedrooms, one or two baths, built to convey a certain cozy American in-town suburban-ness. I knew the guys whose house it was, two brothers from Rose High, popular enough to shine in the firmament but Drama Club enough to have friends who drank and smoked. Their parents were away for the weekend. How the brothers would get the smell of beer and ashtrays out of the shag carpet, I had no idea, but it wasn't my problem either.

One guy randomly walked out of the bathroom, trailing miasma. "Man," he said. "Never eat a whole cucumber all by yourself. It'll give you the *shits*."

"I don't like cucumbers anyway," I said, taking a step back. "But thanks for the tip."

Carl barged in, grabbed a red plastic Solo cup, filled it up at the keg, and wanted to know where Janelle was. I didn't know, myself. Busy boring two or three victims with the "how I got kicked out of NCSSM" story, I couldn't be bothered to keep track of my sister's whereabouts. Someone barged into the bedroom: "Marshall! Somebody told Carl that you're here and you don't approve of him dating your sister! He's gunning for you! You need to hide!"

"What?" This was the late '80s. America has always had an issue with gun violence, but three decades ago it was still rare enough that schoolchildren didn't need body armor. "What are you talking about?"

"He's got a gun!"

And there I was at NCSSM three months earlier trying to feign concern about getting a Level 1 reprimand. What do you do when a drunk redneck who wants to bone your sister and has been told you're there to defend her honor stumbles out to his Camaro to get his gun? In my case, everyone in the room surrounded me, and we barricaded ourselves in the closet. So much for agency. I already knew Janelle had a *vagina dentata* and could fend for herself, probably much better than I could. If worse came to worst, she was probably stoned enough not to feel anything.

In the distance, doors slammed and people shouted. Him: *"Where is he? Where is he?"* Others: "No, man, you don't want to do that." Myself, having had more than enough of my share of the town's bullies, and being one acquainted with the closet, I decided it seemed safest to hang out in there with piles of shoe boxes and clothes and a suitcase or two wedged between us and the door, until everyone else could get rid of the guy. Which they eventually did. We came out again when we heard the roar of his engine and the squeal of the tires.

Welcome back to Greenville.

CHAPTER 22: THE PERILS OF A LITTLE BIT OF MONEY

Freshman year. Okay, so I was technically almost a sophomore already; by the time spring semester 1988 rolled around, I believe I had enough credits to be counted as one, not that it mattered. Those distinctions pertain to people taking the more normal four-year route through college, maybe with a summer session here and there to expedite the process. It didn't take long to make friends: a few guys (Rob Jenkins, Jim Holt, Hank Rudisill) from Honors English, a few more (John Miles, Dav Yaginuma, Jasper Adair, and this guy named Kevin Chaisson we somehow nicknamed Wombat) who lived on their hall in the dorm. Dave Weatherly, one of my kindergarten playmates from New Bern, also turned up at ECU that fall, and we started hanging out again. Now and then I saw the townie Greenville crowd, but most had gone away to other schools, many to State and UNC-Wilmington and Western Carolina. Little beyond reminiscence and proximity connected me to the ones who remained.

I found myself retelling the NCSSM story again, but as time passed, it mattered less. New friendships took the sting out of being at ECU and not someplace more prestigious, and by the end of that year I had decided not to transfer to Carolina once I became eligible. I'd found a measure of balance: I weighed what

I'd been through already against what else I thought I could take. Still separated, not yet divorced, the Marine and Laura fought a two-party war of attrition with increasing rancor and liver damage. Angry at having to pay for my tuition at ECU after apparently assuming all my life he'd get to enjoy the financial freedom offered by whatever full-ride scholarship I accepted, the Marine began withholding child support to repay himself for those expenses. Or so Laura told us. When he refused to pay her what she said he'd agreed to, she sued him, and when he had Janelle and me over to dinner and was out of the room, I'd rummage in his desk for details I could turn over to Laura's lawyer. This was how we learned he and Pam, the woman he'd been seeing, had bought property down at Emerald Isle and were going to build a house. From the blueprints, it looked a lot like the one on King George Road: splondorious. So it wasn't that he couldn't afford to pay for my tuition, it was that he didn't feel he should have to. Brilliant. We'd all then settle at the table and pretend to enjoy the meal. I could tell when Janelle was high: she had a big appetite. And when she was on acid, her pupils were huge and she picked at the food.

I had a choice. I could have transferred away, and probably should have, but I stayed. When I go back over this in my head, I still can't fully explain it. As I wrote in the last paragraph, the decision was partly about weighing what I had (friends, a college experience that was turning out to be better than expected, a certain comfort in familiarity, even the insane kind) against the tumult and anguish of another departure. I'd already said goodbye to and then lost touch with one set of friends. I couldn't do it again, although I'm not sure I could have articulated those feelings then. On top of that, I'd become the center of my family tug-of-war, the only one everyone involved would still talk to. I stayed sober while the rest of them drank and popped pills and took drugs and fell down in restaurants and shouted threats and threw up. I held it together so the rest of them didn't have to. There was the court fight. I learned how to pick locks. I found blueprints. It was a life, or my version of one.

My stories from that year are college stories, not so different from the ones anyone else with a bachelor's degree could tell. Okay, so I was the sober guy who'd have two beers and switch to water so I could drive everybody else home. Drunk, feeling emotional about your girlfriend, and need someone to pick the bigger glass shards out of the back of your hand after you punched the glass in a couple of fire alarms and exposed some bone? I was your guy. I'd drive you to the emergency room, too, and hang out while the doctors stitched you up. Drunk, unconscious, and full of cheap Mexican food that gives you such severe digestive problems that you crap yourself in your sleep and need a gang of friends to haul you to the shower down the hall in the dorm, pull down your shitty underwear, and hose you down? I'm in. Noted around the region as a party school, ECU lived up to its reputation. Every year at Halloween, the town shut down at five. Throughout the City of Greenville, alcohol sales stopped and chains went up over the coolers and across the aisles. If you wanted booze but missed the deadline, you had to drive out of the city limits to Winterville or Bell Arthur. Downtown turned into Mardi Gras in miniature, everyone out in costume and drinking in the streets, open-carry laws be damned. Every year, the gutters literally ran with beer on Halloween night, and that year I finally understood what all the fuss was about.

The day I turned eighteen after that first academic year ended, I went to First Citizens Bank and withdrew the entire amount of my insurance settlement from that car wreck when I was six. After sitting in the bank and earning interest for twelve years, it amounted to almost $9000. Not much by today's standards but kind of a lot back then, especially for an eighteen-year-old with some issues and no idea how to manage sudden money. The bank teller looked at me as if I'd lost my mind when I asked for the whole amount in cash.

"This is Greenville," I said. "What's going to happen?"

Nothing did, except that I went to the State Employees Credit Union, where my bank accounts were, and deposited it there.

The shopping spree got underway without further ado:

First order of business, I had to have a new stereo. I'd been wanting a CD player ever since they'd been invented, and I had resolved to make this happen on the same day I got the money. They'd only been on the market a few years, and although they were no longer seen as luxury items, they were on the expensive side. I bought a pair of good Bose speakers, too, and a receiver. I didn't buy a turntable because Laura had an excellent one sitting unused in a spare closet along with a reel-to-reel tape deck that hadn't been switched on in years.

With the stereo components in my car, I then had to have something to listen to. This worked out to about 30 CDs. On the first shopping trip. These used to cost about US$18 each, so this wasn't a cheap afternoon. In the music store, everyone stopped and stared as I walked the aisles pulling out discs (still in their long cases, a few years before U2 put an end to that form of packaging) and carrying stacks of them in my crossed arms like a geek with his schoolbooks. I bought a mix of my favorite albums as well as a few new releases I'd been holding out for.

"Are you rich?" asked a girl next to me, in a breathless voice.

211

"No," I replied. "It's my birthday."

I paid cash for the CDs and lugged them out to my car, idly wondering how long it would take to open them all later.

Since it was rare to find clothing I liked in Greenville, that weekend I made the first of several shopping runs to Raleigh. The '80s were dying hard in North Carolina: I had to have acid-washed denim (jeans, jacket) and garish neon and shirts with extra pockets and buttons. I'm one of those people clothes never look quite right on, but this didn't bother me then. In the third grade, or possibly the fourth, I had worn the same pair of shoes for an entire school year because the Marine and Laura couldn't afford new ones. You can probably already see where this is going, the kid one generation removed from backwoods Southern poverty, whose parents built the biggest house in the country-club neighborhood but ran out of money before they could finish it.

The car was Laura's idea. The VW had anally birthed its own transmission one night on the way to dinner at the Marine's, and for reasons he declined to share with us, he didn't want me to have his white Datsun hatchback. From somewhere, he got a rattly black 2-door Datsun 210 and gave me the keys. It ran, I'll give it that, but it lacked both air conditioning and the Bug's panache.

I was glad to have the car but Laura kept pointing out how it was a tool he was using against me. Whenever I did something he didn't like, which seemed to be about once a month, he threatened to take it away. Long past tired of his orders and threats, I was starting to suspect the car was less about helping me with transportation and more about finding a way to hang onto control. I had money and a decent part-time job. Why didn't I just buy one for myself, she reasoned, something newer and more reliable? That would put him in his place.

Her cheerleading and his threats were enough to make me check the used-car lots and the want ads. Within a couple of weeks, I was signing the finance papers on a much newer 1983 Nissan Stanza hatchback. White, smooth, and quiet, it was a big improvement over its predecessors. My apprehension about spending that much money quickly subsided. Besides, I could afford it! The loan officer at the SECU had no problem approving the loan; after all, I'd made a sizeable down payment and everyone there knew I had All That Money.

Doubts capered in the back of my mind: how much of Laura's vicarious car-shopping enthusiasm was about striking a blow by proxy in her ongoing fight with the Marine? And when I accepted a pre-approved credit card from Chase Manhattan with a larger credit limit than college students usually got, more than I could comfortably pay back, again, I had some qualms about what I was getting myself into. Not that it stopped me. It wasn't that I was rich, I knew that, but my version of normal had gotten an upgrade.

To make things even more complicated, the squabbles about money and child support took on a new dimension: somehow the Marine had now decided retroactively that the money had *always* been earmarked for college. I don't know where this idea came from or when he first barked it at me. But ours had never been a household in which the family sat down to make rational decisions about matters like these. Apart from Laura's creepy talk about using the settlement to pay for plastic surgery to sand the scar off my cheek, or get a chemical peel, there had been no discussion about the settlement whatsoever. I tended to forget it was there. The closest we'd ever come to having a conversation about how to manage money responsibly was in the second grade, when the Marine and Laura took us to the bank to open our first savings accounts. They gave Janelle and me five dollars each.

"Save some money for a rainy day," the Marine said, and that was the end of that.

We both saved up, although we weren't sure for what, or why we might need cash when it rained. We weren't told these accounts were for college or anything else in particular, just that we needed to have them. No further discussion, no follow-up questions. And as far as I know, people back then didn't start college accounts during the third trimester like they do now. In fairness, there was less tuition-related panic than parents experience today because in-state tuition in North Carolina was much more affordable in 1987: one semester full-time cost about $750, plus another couple hundred for books, less if you could get them secondhand. On a middle-class family's budget, that wasn't dirt-cheap, but it was manageable. Thanks to that car wreck, I had enough money to cover all four years of college. The problem was that no one had ever said I'd need to use it for that purpose... until it was too late, of course.

Reader, I spent it. Every last dime. That summer. I wasn't keeping track because there seemed to be so much of it (everyone kept saying so!) and teenage idiocy is like that. A little bit here, a little bit there, a down payment on a car, a credit card with the balance creeping up toward the red line, a shopping trip to Raleigh every few weeks. I'd stop by Crabtree Valley Mall and buy clothes, then drive over to the area near NC State where there were a number of shops that sold secondhand books and records. On the way home, usually early evening, I'd stop by a repair shop that specialized in old European cars. There were usually a few Citroëns and MGs and Mercedes and BMWs, maybe a Volvo 1800 or a Lancia. Whether they ran or not, I had no idea, but I liked looking at them; they seemed to speak to a world different from and bigger than what Greenville had to offer. And all of a sudden, the money for these respites from boredom and misery was gone. Just like that.

Ever since middle school, I'd been navigating the terrain of major depression. The thing with Steve and my sexuality and What It All Meant took me into some dark places, as did the increasingly scary headlines about the AIDS epidemic. And the ongoing crap with my parents... I suppose I always assumed there'd be enough of the money left in the bank to finance an escape if it came down to that. At the same time, I didn't believe in the future. When I admitted I'd spent all the money, the Marine guffawed at me (in case there was any question about where I learned how to do "forced-sounding laughter") instead of launching into his usual tirade. Which of them arranged the appointment with a psychologist, I have no idea, but I ended up going to see one.

Once.

When I walked into John Rawlins's office, his first question was about my clothing. Why was I wearing a black trench coat and mirrored glasses? He had the same tough-guy bearing as the Marine, so I shut down at once. I mumbled something about liking them. But didn't that mean I was hiding something, that I didn't want the world to see me? Again, the questions like demands and accusations. He asked why I had come to see him, and I explained about NCSSM and then the insurance settlement.

"Let me get this straight," he demanded. "You got... *how much* money? And you spent it all in one summer? Are you *kidding* me?"

Miserable, I nodded.

He burst out laughing, an even harder-edged and more derisive laugh than the Marine's.

"Okay, next question. Are you gay?"

And with that, I was *done*. I hemmed and hawed through the rest of the hour, giving away as little as I could, appalled that he was right about pretty much everything and even more appalled that he was being such a patronizing prick. If I wanted a dose of open scorn from a man my father's age, I already had a father for that. No thank you. Even the relief of leaving didn't help much: I felt a dozen times worse when I left than when I walked into his office. If this was all there was to me, capable in the classroom but a laughable faggot loser in every other respect, I couldn't go on like that and was beginning to think that maybe I shouldn't.

CHAPTER 23: THE FINE YOUNG CANNIBAL

At the beginning of that fall (1988), I dreaded going to Latin IV. For one thing, despite my former "Latin god" status at NCSSM, I had barely passed Latin III the previous semester. The professor, an elderly linguistic genius from some Latin American country, doused us in pedantic contempt. He'd spend half a lecture talking (not ranting, as you might expect, just lecturing as if it were a topic of scholarly interest) about how undisciplined American students were, then ask—seeming truly puzzled— why so many of us skipped class, why so many were getting bad grades. Perhaps more than the other students, I annoyed him. I'd placed into Latin III. I was several years younger than everyone else in the class, bright and linguistically capable. Why didn't I seem to give a damn? I didn't know how to tell him how offensive his pedantic tirades were, not just to me but to the whole class; I just kept my head down and got through the lessons with the minimum effort necessary. The first day of Latin IV, I wore black. In fact, that became my ritual at the start of every new semester: I wore black.

This time, there were two unfamiliar people in the room: a young (and unusually handsome) guy about my own age. In front of him, down at the bottom of the lecture hall next the professor's lectern, sat a woman in an unflattering navy blue smock.

When the woman in the blue smock raised her hands and started signing to the new guy, I was floored. So, apparently, was everybody else. My first reaction: *Oh wow, so he's deaf, and he placed into Latin IV… he's got to be smart as hell. Now I've really got to talk to him.*

That first day, I was seated by the door and had a good view of them both. I couldn't take my eyes off them. The sign-language part fascinated me, of course. I'd seen it on TV every so often, but never up close like this. But the new guy. He was obviously a freshman, seeing the room and its occupants for the first time, recognizing nothing and none of us. He was kind of hot, too, despite his ridiculous fluorescent orange windbreaker. I hadn't quite begun to allow myself to think of other men in sexual terms, or to acknowledge it as such, but that's how I reacted to him. I wanted to keep him in sight; I wanted to talk to him—*This is a boring class, the professor's an asshole, and the other students are about as exciting as a heap of broken mannequins in the back room of a department store*—but I couldn't summon any pretext.

Next class, two days later, I contrived to be late. Since I'm not punctual by nature, this wasn't hard. The only available seat was next to him, and I took it. As discreetly as possible, I struck up a conversation by writing a note: *Who's she?* I drew an arrow pointing toward the woman in the navy smock.

My interpreter?, he wrote.

Yes.

She's my interpreter. I'm deaf, so she's signing what the professor says.

I wrote, *In Latin?*

Yes.

Impressive. I wasn't quite consciously aware of the fact that I wanted to get in his pants, but the revelation wasn't far off. Adam looked like a younger, skinnier version of Roland Gift, the lead singer for the Fine Young Cannibals. (This was 1988. They were at their peak then.) Adam also exuded charisma, not from anything he consciously did; it was something pheromonal, perhaps, or some ineffable mix of good looks, confidence, and subtle look-at-me body language. (Today we would call it Big Dick Energy.) In the coming weeks, we starting hanging out, and I learned he'd been adopted. No idea who his biological parents were. When I asked about his race, he didn't know that either. The full lips, the shape of his face, the olive skin, and the fine, tightly curled brown hair suggested a black parent or grandparent; so did his light green eyes. His best friend Warren's mom was Mexican, and the idea of a Latin connection had also been proposed. He usually told people he was part American Indian, not because he was (or even knew) but because it was expedient. But officially, he was white; his adoptive parents were white; and after a certain point, it was useless to speculate.

One night not long after the start of the spring semester, we got caught in the rain. Adam had moved off campus already; he couldn't stand the dorm, couldn't study there. Determined to graduate valedictorian, as he had done at his high school, he talked his parents into renting him an apartment near campus. We'd just gone for a walk to the convenience store up the street. Typical eastern North Carolina weather happened: clouds rolled in, obscuring the stars, and within minutes it was pouring. Neither of us had an umbrella. We waited in the ATM alcove at a nearby bank for the rain to let up; when it did, we dashed back to his flat. Not drenched when we got there, but damp enough to need towels, we stood in his kitchen for a long, delicious moment looking at each other. This was my first authentic experience with sexual tension—the mutual kind, not its unrequited counterpart made up mostly of blue balls and teenage delusions. I had never wanted to kiss someone so badly before, not even Steve. With him, that vibe had never been there. Not like this. For the first time in my life, it occurred to me that Adam might have been feeling the same thing in that moment. Nothing happened, of course. After an excruciating moment, he went to the bathroom to get a couple of towels. He had a few beers in the fridge; we drank those and carried on as if nothing had happened.

After that, it didn't take long for me to come crashing out of the closet. Some background: I hadn't learned ASL yet, I was too self-conscious to use the few signs I'd picked up, and I didn't have even a fraction of the vocabulary I needed for that conversation. Mostly we talked by writing notes to each other.

I wanted to hang out one Friday night a few weeks later. He had plans with one of the other deaf students on campus, a junior I already knew was gay. They were going to the Paddock Club, Greenville's long-running gay bar. All through high school, that club had been part of the taunting: "Are you going to the Paddock Club this weekend?" "You didn't get invited to such-and-such's party? Probably didn't matter, since you were going to the Paddock Club anyway." Shit like that. And he was going there?

Why? I wrote, more shaken than horrified.

He looked at me for a long time before replying. Those odd green eyes seemed to be saying, *You idiot, isn't it obvious?*

When the light bulb didn't blink on over my head, he picked

up the pad and wrote, *Because I'm bi. I like guys too.*

The words set off an EMP in my brain, a bright white blast that fried everything. I performed nonchalance or tried to. By then, I'd already come to grasp a bit about how observant deaf people are. Unlike Laura, wrapped up in her own mesh of stories and lies and feigning empathy by telling me what I felt instead of asking, Adam actually could see right through me. One glance and he could tell if I needed to go to the bathroom or was annoyed about something or needed to eat. It only seemed uncanny until I met the other deaf students. They were all like that. How much time passed between that EMP detonation and me coming out too, I can't say. It was a matter of days, not weeks or months. I remember none of it.

Coming out of the daze, I went to see *The Accidental Tourist* one Sunday afternoon. I hadn't read the original Anne Tyler novel and knew nothing about the story. I suppose I was expecting New York and Paris, maybe Rome or Rio. The sugary domestic quirkiness set up a horror-ricochet in my head: I could not live my life like these characters. Angst over a marriage that wasn't working out. Shafts of winter-pale sunlight in dark rooms where dust hung in the air. I could almost smell the mothballs and suffocation. Now, almost thirty years later, the details are gone but the impressions remain. This would be my life if I didn't do something about it. Numb, I drove over to my friend Alice's apartment hoping for a dose of sanity and ended up getting the opposite.

I had met Alice during freshman orientation. Before that, I had never met anyone from such a conservative background. Her deeply traditional hopes for marriage to her boyfriend Ray had begun to depress me, so I'm not sure what made me think stopping by would be the best idea. As far as she was concerned, it was a foregone conclusion that they'd get married. She liked it when he ordered her to do this or that, because she'd been raised with the view that women should be subservient to men. She didn't even mind if he hit her, as long as it wasn't too hard. She viewed it as correction. That's how God wanted it.

We drank tea and she talked about her job at the diner where she was working now that she had dropped out of ECU. She was saving $7 per week toward the wedding, never mind that Stan had dumped her and was now only seeing her again on a conditional basis.

"One day you'll be a famous writer, and you'll come visit Ray and me in our home in Raleigh," she said.

Gratifying, but I noticed the implicit assumption that I would be single. I thought of the excess of dark wood in *The Accidental Tourist*. Silent rooms, bleak Carolina winters, pine trees creaking outside. Alice's apartment, with its fussy Southern college-girl decorations and doilies, depressed me almost as much as the movie sets had. Time ground to a halt in houses like this. It trapped people in them.

This is what my life is heading for if I don't do something about it now.

I made some excuse and fled the apartment.

My initial temptation was to track Adam down. I suppose I was still reeling from his revelation that he was bi. He had been so calm about it, as he was about most things. But he was on the other side of campus, and was likely to have his nose in a book. He was triple-majoring in biology, chemistry, and biochemistry, and was determined to graduate valedictorian and go on to medical school, not because he particularly wanted to be a doctor but because he thought he needed to prove the point that a deaf guy could do these things. (He succeeded.) Ergo, his nose was always in a book. It wouldn't have been the best idea for me to see him, anyway: I didn't know how to articulate all the screaming static in my head. If I tried to talk to him about it, I'd look insane. I felt insane. Plus, I had a strong sense that he was also the *last* person I needed to see at that moment. It wasn't just that he'd be busy, either. I didn't quite know why yet, but I listened to this instinct.

Alice's apartment was at the edge of downtown Greenville, a few blocks away from the Tar River. I drove across it, turned left on the airport road, and doubled back toward the Swamp, a patch of undeveloped land that surrounded a series of ponds just south of West Meadowbrook Park. Some friends and I had discovered the place during our first year. A series of hiking trails led through it, but no one ever seemed to use them, and you could climb up on the railroad tracks and walk across the trestle bridge over the river, back into downtown. You'd be fucked if a train ever came, but they rumbled through town only once or twice a day. In the logic of university students, this was a hangout par excellence. I needed to be absolutely alone for a while, and the vague sense of risk sweetened the moment. I parked, looked around, got out, walked back toward the river, and climbed the tumble of rocks beside the railroad track.

I walked out to the midpoint and looked down at the dark water.

To my right: Greenville's height-restricted cityscape, too modest to be called a skyline. Light reflected orange-grey off low clouds. Later in the year, I'd say they were snow clouds, but it was barely fall; cold weather (inasmuch as eastern North Carolina gets cold) wouldn't arrive for another couple of months. Ahead of me: darkness. The single railroad track ran north, out of the city. I had no idea where it ultimately went. Past farms and tobacco fields and little towns like Bethel. Down below: the river. Although it probably wasn't deep, I knew from years of swimming what the impact would be like. From this height, my body would slap the water hard enough to break bones. I was still a good enough swimmer that drowning wouldn't be likely under normal circumstances, but these weren't normal circumstances.

I can't go on living like this, I thought. *I can't keep feeling like I'm full of tangled knots. I've been like this all my life and I can't keep doing it. I can't stand it. I can't stand not being able to stand myself.*

The long periods of blankness. The years of being bullied. A lifetime of being told who I was, without ever getting a chance to find out for myself. My whole life seemed to come down to this one thing, this one word: faggot. Whether it was the Marine throwing me in the pond in a fit of disgust, Laura sneering after a questionable-looking waiter left our table, or some bully vandalizing my bike or my locker, there it was. Faggot. If it hadn't gone away yet, it probably wasn't going to.

I can't go on living like this. I can't go on hating myself.

I stayed up on the bridge for a long time, looking down at the water.

There's so much wrong with my life, and I never asked for any of it. What the hell did I do?

It all sounds melodramatic now, but when you're eighteen and consciously acknowledging for the first time that your entire existence is predicated on a series of lies, it's traumatic. "Melotraumatic" probably isn't a word but it ought to be. From my psychology classes and my own reading (every gay kid surreptitiously seeks out information, either in the library or online), I knew sexual orientation wasn't a chosen trait, and it certainly wasn't a lifestyle. But this knowledge had never translated into ease. I was at an endpoint: either the agony had to end or I did.

The truth was like a whisper audible above the din inside of me: *I'm not straight*. I wasn't ready for the G word yet, and wouldn't be for another year and a half or so. There are layers upon layers of truth: endless sub-basements, corridors of locked doors. This was as much as I could handle, as far as I could go. *I'm not straight*. For the first time, I let myself imagine having a boyfriend and not a girlfriend.

Adam said he was bi. That must mean I was bi too. Or something.

I might be happier.

I thought more. I began to walk back to the car.

What could happen to me that hasn't already happened? How could it possibly be worse than what I've already been through?

What was the point of further denial when I'd still be called names anyway? In fact, that seemed to be the fulcrum upon which the entire problem pivoted. Most of my denial was about other people's disgust, about not wanting to be reduced to that one damning word. I resisted the truth because I didn't want a whole lifetime of people to be right. I'd been force-fed the wrong information all my life, taught I was something and someone I really wasn't.

I looked down at the churning black water a little while longer.

No, I wasn't going to jump.

It was a start.

CHAPTER 24: WE'RE ALL CRIMINALS NOW

There was always more to Granny than met the eye. Always a bit plump from a diet her doctor described as mostly "Coca-Cola and sow-belly," she liked to buy nondescript station wagons with big engines so that she could speed and cry old-lady crocodile tears if she ever got stopped. My lead foot is a genetic affliction. The summer between my junior and senior years at S&M, the Marine got mad at me for getting a speeding ticket while driving his car to Durham to see Steve. As if that weren't enough, the phone bill came. I had charged a few of my long-distance calls to Steve to the Marine's account (you could do that back then). When both of these things happened within a couple of days of each other, a huge mound of shit hit the fan. Fair enough, I had it coming, but this time the Marine's brown frenzy took on a new form. He started barking demands: I was to come over the following Saturday and do a long list of yard work to repay him. He'd be out of town, but every item on this list had damn well better be finished, or it would be Katy bar the door. Mow the lawn. Trim Granny's azalea hedges. Pull up the (rare) irises she had cultivated over the years. (Granny had planted so many flowers that her house was featured on the evening news once.) The Marine raved on and on, bellowing whatever popped into his head, so much so—and making so little sense—that I let Laura listen in. She then called Granny. I didn't hear all of it, but after they had conferred, Laura came back to me and said, "He's lost his goddamn mind. There's no way you're doing all that. There's no way you even could. Not in one day. You should mow the lawn, because you *did* charge those calls to him, and then we'll see."

Granny already detested him for leaving, and now, as she saw it, he wanted me to destroy her garden for no other reason than because it was too flowery and so was I. She wasn't having it. I had no idea how angry she was until Laura and I picked her up that Saturday morning. Southern ladies of her generation can smile as they slice off your face, but she was past that. Even if age had turned her hair an indeterminate hue between blonde and grey, she maintained her redheaded fury. That morning, she said very little. She'd put her false teeth in, but her mouth was a lipless white line of wordless rage. Instead of talking, she walked around the yard, perhaps saying a quiet goodbye.

As promised, I mowed the lawn. It didn't take long. The house, a two-bedroom bungalow from the '30s, sat on a very small lot. Laura and Granny busied themselves trimming the azaleas and hydrangeas, just enough to make it look as if work had been done. Then it was time to deal with the flowerbeds. They dug up a few of the irises Granny could not bear to lose; we'd transplant them to our own yard. Even that took effort: their rhizomes had grown and spread, and uprooting all of them would have taken several days. When that was done, Granny went on the warpath.

"He doesn't like my irises?" she asked rhetorically. "Then I want you to take that lawnmower and mow them to the damn ground. And then we're leaving."

"You're sure?"

She mulled it over for a moment and said, "If he doesn't like it, he can go straight to hell."

"After this," Laura said. "You're not to talk to him. We will."

I hated doing it, but the fuck-you more than made up for the act of mass iricide. Nothing further was said after that, but at least there were no more demands for me to come over and do physical labor.

When I was in college, Granny's streak of lawlessness continued. The older she got, the fewer fucks she had to give. One afternoon during my freshman year when I stopped by for a visit, she gestured at a silver ceramic cat she was using as a doorstop. Her apartment had so much bric-a-brac that apart from her sewing table there was no vacant shelf space.

"There's $50,000 inside of that cat," she said. An old fellow who lived down the hall used to drive getaway cars for various local criminal undertakings and needed a secure place to stash his money in case he died and the wrong set of relatives stopped by to search his flat for ill-gotten loot. A safe deposit box would have been the more logical place for it, but their generation had lived through the Depression and didn't trust banks. With glee, she added, *"I stuffed his wad inside of my pussy!"*

As a kid, I never fully understood Granny and Sam, the man she sort of lived with. She was a widow and he was a much older man who seemed to have a lot of money despite the modesty of their homes. They lived in their own trailers on a huge lot in New Bern. He owned the land, the three trailers (the third was rented out), and the huge corrugated metal warehouse that had housed our secondhand store for a couple of years. Each of them had their own trailer. Sam's was an odd shade between yellow and beige, inside and out. He liked the light dim and didn't go out much. He spent most of his days lying on the sofa with the air conditioning on high. Naps, Mountain Dew, and *Playboy* magazines kept him going, and Granny cooked for them both. Her own trailer, green and white, with splendid '70s wood paneling and shag carpet, was its own little parallel universe of old-lady weirdness. She kept all her sewing paraphernalia in the front bedroom: boxes and boxes of needles and thread, skeins of yarn, jars of buttons. Two dress forms with knobs you could crank to make the boobs bigger. (As kids, we were easily amused.) The lot must have been two acres of grass and loblolly pines, and I read book after book in a hammock strung up between two of those trees.

According to Laura's stories and the bits I could intuit from what she left out, Sam had, like Granny's two brothers Brian and Clyde, been a rum-runner back in Prohibition. The swampy waterways of the Outer Banks and the inland coastal counties lent themselves well to all kinds of crimes. After booze became legal again, they branched out into other forms of smuggling. At any given time, he had barrels and barrels of illicit gasoline stashed in the back, just waiting to explode. (Back in the crazy inflation days of the '70s, this actually wasn't such an insane idea if he could buy the stuff cheap.) I suppose I thought of Sam as what we would now call a sugar daddy: he was kind of rich, and Granny was kind of his lady friend, even if they weren't romantically involved. She once sort of randomly said (I really have no idea where this came from), "Sam wanted me to do *oralsex* on him, and I just wouldn't. I *couldn't*! Can you *imagine*?" (As it turned out, I could. Not with him, of course, but by the time I was eighteen or so, I was spending quite a lot of time imagining doing that.) Those undercurrents aside, they seemed to be happy, and there was always money. Hundred-dollar bills surreptitiously passed across the table. Envelopes of cash to finance family trips the Marine and Laura couldn't have afforded on their own. Looking back, I think it was less about wealth and more about living well below their means, but when I was a kid, I thought we weren't rich, exactly, but... rich-adjacent.

Granny always had her own brand of lunacy, having grown up in deeply rural Hyde County in the early 20th century. She told stories about having to share one tub of bathwater. Being the oldest of her four siblings, she got to take her baths first. Clyde, the youngest, always got the cold, dirty water. Having visited Clyde's ramshackle house in Swan Quarter—a two-story, turn-of-the-century clapboard structure I now think withstood hurricanes and flooding mostly by virtue of its sieve-like permeability—I understood these privations: the house only had running water on the ground floor, and there were chamber pots upstairs in case you needed to relieve yourself in the night. I remember being about four and hoping I'd need to take a shit because I thought it would be fun to point my butt at the pot. Married to Dick, a man much older than herself, a relic from the Victorian era, she must have been in a constant tug-of-war between the modernity she saw emerging and the constant backward force he represented. She developed a certain thick-skinned, no-nonsense bluntness, and once widowed did whatever she goddamn wanted.

It's easy for me to point out where I got my foul mouth, my love of driving too fast, and my utter lack of interest in the rules. I also know where Laura got her crazy. Granny had no filter either. When we were kids, this was charming. If one of us farted, she'd chirp "There's more room out than there is in!" or "The fox is the finder, the scent is behind her!" and that would be that.

In retirement, she took a job as a nanny for a prominent attorney in Greenville. The attorney, whom I should probably not name, had two young kids and a growing law practice and needed full-time help. I don't know whose idea the salary arrangements were, but Granny ended up working for less than minimum wage and getting paid in cash. She didn't want to report the income and risk her Social Security benefits, and the attorney wanted to save a few bucks, but I wouldn't go so far as to say it was a win-win situation. It was, as nearly as I could tell, one more situation in which a Southern woman of a certain age had to perform normality. In public, she was a kindly and somewhat overweight elderly woman. Behind closed doors, she'd scream things like *"Get your big fat ass off that table!"* at the kids when they got too rambunctious.

She had her own brand of crazy. The cartoonist B. Kliban, whose work I loved as a kid (how could I not?), once did a one-frame cartoon titled "Exhibit Your Symptom." In a satire of an American talk show or game show, a beak-nosed host with a grin like a shark presides over a line of people in various states of undress. A big-butted cameraman films the scene. Whenever Granny had a sore on her calf or a bruise on her arm, she'd perform absentmindedness as she rolled up her pants leg or her sleeve so that we could see. The intention, of course, was to provoke comment, sympathy, attention. This lack of a filter sometimes went too far. I once saw her in her back yard with one side of her shirt up, in conversation with the neighbor whose garden abutted her own.

"A young man is coming," said the neighbor woman just as I passed into earshot.

Granny put her shirt down again. I didn't want to know

what had compelled her to pull out a boob in a chat with her neighbor, and didn't ask. Another time, she told the story of her hysterectomy, an emergency procedure. It was the holidays and the doctor showed up reeking of booze and cigarette smoke. Against her protests, he put her under; as the ether took her, she slipped into the dark scared she wouldn't wake up. She did, later, in pain. As she put it, he "removed a pound and a half of proud flesh from the opening in my body." To code-switch back to English, the doctor fucked something up and left her insides full of scar tissue.

I grew up knowing it sometimes took crazy to handle crazy, and the day the Marine- and Laura's divorce was finalized, Laura came home from court, went to bed, and started screaming. She hadn't noticed my car and didn't realize I was still in bed, myself. Or perhaps she did. She was born for the stage. Her screams of "I WANT TO DIE! I WANT TO DIE! I WANT TO DIE! PLEASE LET ME DIE!" woke me up. For a time, I stayed in bed, listening. When she didn't stop screaming, I started to panic. Would she actually do it? There was a gun in the house and her favorite topics of conversation were her will and her suicide plan in case of a diagnosis with a terminal disease. And her revelation that she and the Marine had planned to shoot Janelle and me in our sleep in the event of a nuclear war was never far from my mind.

As quietly as possible, I got up, went to her bedroom, and sat down on the bed next to her. This brought on a paralysis of some sort: she stopped screaming, lay perfectly still, and wouldn't respond to my questions. I shook her gently. No response. I tried again. No response. So I called Granny from the phone in the kitchen: "It's Mom. Divorce court was today, she got home and started screaming, and now she's like, frozen or something. Can you come over and make her snap out of it? I can't."

Granny got there in less than twenty minutes. (That's one perk of living in a small town.) She shut Laura's bedroom door behind her but the house was small enough that I could her version of tough love: Your life isn't over. You have the kids. Life goes on. Stop crying like a little tittybaby and act like a grown woman with kids. This isn't the end, he was a shithead, carry on. Words to that effect.

That episode passed, as they do, and since she also later lost the court case about him withholding money from her child support, naturally before long—sophomore year, maybe junior—the conversations turned to the subject of killing him. This was not, of course, the kind of thing I talked to Jim and Hank and Dav and Adam about. "Hey, what's up? Bud or Michelob Dry?" "Michelob Dry. So we're talking about killing my father. Should we have him shot or arrange a hit-and-run?" It was the South. Granny knew people, or her brothers did. Accidents could be made to happen. I can't say any of this surprises me in retrospect, and it would be a lie to say I entirely disapproved at the time. One night after a beating, I stood over him holding the largest knife from the kitchen. I must have been about ten then, maybe eleven. While he snored, I mulled over where to stab him, knowing I'd only get one chance. He'd survived worse in Vietnam and it had turned him into a bellowing skin full of violence. It would have to be the jugular or nothing, and I couldn't go through with it, not just because I was afraid I'd screw it up and he'd live but because the bullying and butt rape in the reform school I'd be sent to would be worse. Another time, I was holding onto a nylon strap to help maintain his support as he repaired rusty spots on the roof of the warehouse in New Bern. "If you let go, you're gonna be scraping me off the driveway," he said. I looked down and did the math. We weren't high enough. If he'd survived someone sabotaging his jet, a fall from this height wouldn't do much useful damage. I might have been about ten, but I could put two and two together in my head without needing to show my work. Besides, I sort of understood then that no matter how bad the beating and the bullying got, I could always look back later and remind myself that certain people were alive because I had allowed it. I saw the path and chose not to go down it. It's dark therapy, but effective.

In the end, a version of sanity prevailed. Revenge talk is a good salve for a broken heart. Enacting it warrants more scrutiny. On the rare occasions after that when Granny saw the Marine, she'd cut him dead with a look and a few choice words. As was the case in the two years before going to S&M, I began to see that although ECU had turned out much better than I'd expected, there was no way I could stay in Greenville much past graduation. If this was the kind of drama I'd find myself drawn into again, I was going to have to leave, whatever it took.

234

CHAPTER 25: THE WASHINGTON MONUMENT

Oddly enough, it would take another year after I came out before I actually did anything about it. I wanted to, but it felt as if I'd just touched down in a foreign country. The ink of my passport stamp was still wet, I didn't know where anything was, I didn't have a map or a guidebook, and there was a grand total of two people I could ask for directions. For the time being, it was enough to *imagine* doing stuff with guys, to allow myself to be intrigued and turned on. I'd had enough of revulsion.

The Internet wasn't around then, not to any useful extent, so I couldn't go online to find information and guys. The first person I told was, of course, Adam, who promptly freaked out. I'd put a lot of effort into convincing him I was straight, and when I told him, he didn't take it well, didn't want the icky, annoying emotional responsibility of having someone "come out on him," as he put it. Several weeks later, I drove to Blacksburg, Virginia (about seven hours each way) to tell Heath Hart in person. Being a few years older and considerably more gracious than Adam, Heath was also a great deal more sanguine. After his surprise wore off and he'd assured himself I wasn't playing a bizarre prank, he said, "There's one thing you should keep in mind. After you come out, there's no going back in. No one will believe you."

There was no risk of that whatsoever. Imagine the relief after finally getting effective treatment for a chronic-pain condition you've had for years. Having gotten used to the broken glass in your hips or your kneecaps, you keep noticing the absence of pain and exulting in it. So yeah, even if I'd never so much as kissed a guy before, there was no going back.

You might think the Paddock Club would have been my first gay bar, but that's not how it happened. Still unwilling to set foot in the place for fear of whom I might bump into, I changed nothing about my previous social life. I had the same circles of friends, most of which didn't overlap. Even for a raging introvert like me, there were one or two other non-concentric circles because college is like that. I was busy enough not to feel as if I lacked anything. Well, except for a boyfriend. Or any sexual experience whatsoever of the kind I was craving.

Eventually Adam suggested we go to DC for a long weekend. Traffic's probably much worse now, but it used to be a four-hour drive from Greenville if you had a lead foot, which I did. (I've done it in three hours and forty, door to door.) I'd never been to a gay bar before, but I'd already learned this was how gay nightlife worked. Friday night, you stayed in Greenville. Saturday night, when the Paddock was dead, you went somewhere else: Raleigh, Durham, Jacksonville, Wilmington, even Greensboro. (Norfolk and Virginia Beach were closer than Greensboro, and Richmond was about the same distance, but some psychological barrier kept people from crossing the state line.) Two other friends of ours, Warren and Torrence, came along as well. Warren, Adam's best friend, also deaf, was one of those straight guys so comfortable in his own skin that nothing perturbed him. Torrence, a few years older, had been out much

236

longer and seen it all and would theoretically keep us from doing anything stupid.

The day we arrived, we stopped by Gallaudet University to walk around. Adam and Warren had a couple of friends there. Amazed that there was a university for deaf people, and still not very fluent in ASL (Torrence was much better), I tried not to gawk at everyone and everything. (If you had told me I'd end up working there and living on campus just six years later, I wouldn't have believed you.) For the first time, I could almost picture my life on its own trajectory, one delinked from Laura's day-to-day craziness and the Marine's orders and threats. After the campus visit, we stopped in nearby Union Station to browse around. Unprepared for the grandeur of the place, I gawked more and said little. In fact, that seemed to set that tone for the trip: New Orleans was the only other major city I'd visited with that type of urban density. I'd never been on a subway before; the closest I'd come was the historic streetcar that ran between the Garden District and the French Quarter. Washington's metro stations are dim, cylindrical vaults underground—new (then) tiles on the station floors, recessed lighting, shiny silver trains quietly roaring into the stations and out again. Circular lights on the edge of the platform that blinked when a train was about to arrive, a futuristic detail that kept reminding me I wasn't just four hours away from eastern North Carolina, I was four parsecs away.

My first gay club was Tracks, a cavernous space down in a part of Southeast DC where if you didn't get mugged or shot on the way from your car to the venue, you could call the night a success. I didn't know this at the time. If I had, I'd have gone anyway. I'd done enough reading to know that gay bars tended to be found in the rougher edges of town, the peripheries. The

Paddock Club was in the same kind of neighborhood back in Greenville, albeit not as dangerous. It was tucked away in the back half of the building that housed the local Harley-Davidson dealership.

Being me, I required a couple of Pepto-Bismol tabs to keep from having to use the bathroom three or four times before we left the hotel. Or, more likely, I had to use the bathroom three or four times before we left the hotel and finally popped some pills so that I could spend the night somewhere more interesting than Howard Johnson's. We piled into Adam's CRX. Somehow all four of us fit (I think Warren sat on Torrence's lap and I curled up in the back), and it wasn't actually that far from our hotel. We paid our admission at the door and trooped in. Music pounded. My entire body vibrated. I hoped the pink tablets would hold.

I wasn't sure what I was expecting, but what I got was, well, a bunch of gay guys standing around talking to each other, not so different from the couple of parties I'd been to but on a much larger scale. Deafening music, but then, I could more or less express myself in ASL by that point, so it didn't matter. Adam and Warren liked the noise because it felt good. We wandered from one part of the club to the next, checking the place out. Had I ever been in a nightclub at all before this, any nightclub? I don't think that I had. Strobe lights pulsed. Taut, shirtless bodies writhed on the dance floor. A commingled smell of beer and sweat and other odors I couldn't identify hung in the air. You could still smoke indoors then, and the air was thick with it. I hated the smell, hated the way it made my eyes sting, but there was no escaping it.

I could talk to one of these guys, I marveled. We could hit it off. I could go home with him. Nothing was going to happen with Adam, whom I still found attractive but whose reaction when I came out had put me off. But there might be some interesting guy with the same broken china in his head: we'd have an intense conversation over a couple of beers, go back to his apartment, have a couple more, and… you know.

It didn't happen. Not that night, anyway.

We visited a couple of the Smithsonian museums that Saturday. The Museum of Natural History, I think. Dinosaur bones and the Hope Diamond. That night, we went to a few of the bars on P Street in Dupont Circle (which used to be DC's gayborhood), both smaller venues, crowded, dark. Quick trip through Friends. Too many people. ASL doesn't work if you're jammed up against the people you're trying to talk to. We had just walked into the second one, Badlands (how many bars and clubs have had that name?) when someone grabbed my arm. A black guy. Interesting.

Are you deaf?, he signed, a bit awkwardly (not that I was much better).

My reply: *No, I'm hearing, but my friends are deaf.*

He misunderstood me, thought I said I was deaf (it *was* rather dark in there), and kept signing. Which was just as well, since the music made talking rather difficult. Adam, Warren, and Torrence sort of collectively raised an eyebrow at me and kept going.

Do you want a drink?

I fingerspelled *GIN AND TONIC*.

Part of me wanted to join the others. There was (let's be honest) that inevitable moment of Southern Racism Processing to get through. You can't grow up steeped in it and eradicate all the prejudices that have soaked in just by deciding you don't want them anymore and poof they're gone. It takes more work than that. No matter how good my intentions were, I had no grasp of how much there still was to learn. In the year since I'd come out, I'd had all kinds of fantasies about who my first guy would be, what that first experience would be like, who I might meet in the future. These always involved white men. Greenville was predominantly white and black: the Latino population hadn't arrived yet, not to any significant degree, and there were like twenty Asians in the whole city. It had never crossed my mind that I might meet a cool black guy. Until I did. He was shorter than me (which I liked), not bad-looking, taut in a way that white guys are not. The big Bambi eyes were very appealing. I began thinking impure thoughts.

He came back with my drink and tried to sign something else. When I leaned forward and said, "I can hear you," he looked so offended that I felt awful. "I said my *friends* are deaf," I insisted. "I'm not!"

Being an arrogant bastard (I've known him thirty years now and am allowed to say this), Don refused to believe he'd misunderstood me. We introduced ourselves again, and suddenly I didn't want to join the others. Of course it felt unreal—my entire life felt unreal and still does—but I could feel the people bumping into me, hear the bass pounding against my eardrums, taste the astringent gin and tonic as I finished my second one, and then a third (I didn't tell him until later that I was two years shy of being legal). Somehow we managed to have a conversation in that noisy place, and I began to see that he liked me *because* I was an awkward blond dork and not in spite of it.

Let's cut to the chase. I drove us back to his place. It didn't bother me that I was probably a little too drunk to drive. The upside of having parents who were hammered as often as the Marine and Laura was a pretty good alcohol tolerance. (Okay, better than pretty good. Terrifying.) Besides, DC barely had a working government then: garbage piled up on street corners like Naples, you could park wherever you wanted and throw the tickets away, and who knew where the cops were? Priorities were priorities: this guy actually wanted to get in my pants, and I needed to do whatever it goddamn took in order to make that happen.

Don lived in an English basement flat in the rowhouses on F Street NE, several blocks east of Union Station and south of Gallaudet. His apartment made me more nervous than he did: a matching sofa and armchairs with dark rosewood and stiff upholstery, framed artwork on the walls instead of the college-boy posters I was used to. Everything looked expensive. He had money and I'd spent all of mine; I was a junior in college, mostly broke, and delivering pizzas to earn extra cash. My coworkers at Domino's and I smoked a lot of weed and sometimes got high with our stoner customers and shared the food they'd ordered. One time I left a lit joint on the dashboard of the delivery truck and it melted a hole in the plastic. Best not to talk about this. He couldn't possibly want me, but yet, there we were in his living room.

Kissing another man for the first time when you're gay and you've never done that before and you've spent a year waiting to get laid and (bonus!) you're really into him… it was a primal moment of *Holy shit, I get it now.* I'd had sex with girls before. I fumbled through it and mistook the relief I felt afterward for pleasure. For the first time, I was kissing someone with razor stubble. If there had ever been a bigger turn-on in the history of sex, I couldn't have told you what it was, at least not until my hands went roaming and one ended up on the Washington Monument in his pants. Somehow I managed not to come then and there. You know where this is going, so I'll spare you the pornography. Clichés be damned, I had to bite the pillow to keep from waking the upstairs neighbors with all the noise I'd otherwise have been making.

Unfortunately, these fireworks all led to him thinking I was actually good in bed. I wasn't. It was a mad cocktail of gin, enthusiasm, and beginner's luck. I spent the night with him, and we made plans to meet up again in a couple of weeks; I'd drive up on my own.

It didn't last long. Six years older and vastly more experienced than me, he got bored fast. He'd been in the Army and was stationed in Germany, so he spoke good German in addition to Spanish and French. He had a job doing something IT-related. He'd been out for years and shagged any number of men. The problem with having sex with a cute awkward drunk gay dork is that after the first couple of times, the dork is sober, the novelty of the cuteness wears thin, and there's still the awkwardness to contend with. After a few months, he'd had enough and dumped me.

It didn't take long for Laura to find out about him, because naturally she had convinced herself that it was okay to eavesdrop on our phone calls and ransack our rooms when we went out. Long used to doorknobs with locks that mysteriously broke and never seemed to get fixed, I sort of assumed she was doing that. But then, I was also used to the idea. I'd outgrown the belief that she had Janelle and me under telepathic surveillance, of course. That was bullshit. Still, somehow I wasn't quite prepared when she confronted me:

"So, I overheard your sister talking to her friend, and she said you were having a homosexual affair... *with a black man!* I just didn't believe it at first. I thought it was some kind of joke.

242

I just couldn't believe you would... *do that to me!*" She looked at me, tears welling in her eyes. "I had to go straight to the counseling center on campus after that, because I just couldn't believe it could be true. I just..."

"You were eavesdropping," I said. "You didn't just happen to overhear that."

"Be that as it may."

"You went through my things, too, didn't you?"

She looked down, and the tears spilled down her cheeks. After a moment, she looked up again and screamed, "I HAD A RIGHT TO! HOW COULD YOU EVEN *THINK* ABOUT DOING SOMETHING LIKE THAT? *I HAVE A RIGHT TO GRANDCHILDREN!*"

"Oh dear God." I borrowed a line Don sometimes used: "This conversation is terminated."

More screaming ensued.

"I'm going out," I snapped. "Before I go, two things. One: I am not dating anybody. Two: If I am, it's none of your business. Grow up."

I don't remember where I went. The more unhinged she became, the farther away I'd drive, sometimes out into the surrounding countryside, once all the way to the beach. When I got home, she'd gone to bed, and an empty jug of white wine told me she'd had help.

Having been raised on a diet of histrionics and cognitive dissonance, I understood a few things without being told. No matter how much she screamed, she wouldn't throw me out for being gay. I knew that happened to other kids, but with the Marine gone and Janelle increasingly vocal about her plans to move out on her eighteenth birthday, Laura's need for attention would eclipse her homophobia. I also understood that I'd run out of money. Now paying my tuition with student loans (fortunately, it was cheap back then) and earning minimum wage ($3.35 per hour) at various part-time jobs, I didn't have many options. The dorms? No, after S&M I decided I was done walking down the hall to use a dirty communal bathroom, and now that I'd come out, I had residual worries about being the Big Fag on the Hall.

No, the best way to deal with her was—now that Janelle and I were older—to shame her for not acting her age. In her drunken hysterics after the divorce, she had abdicated adulthood. She had also kept us as naïve as possible for as long as possible, not wanting us to surpass her own maturity level. I knew exactly what I was doing when I chose to stay, I knew why I was doing it, and I knew what the cost would be to us both—the cost I would pay as well as the one I would inflict. More than that, I finally understood why the Marine had left. I think I always had, or at least been able to see the outline; now I realized I didn't blame him for it, or not as much as I had. A small milestone, but one I needed to speed past on the way to wherever else I was going.

CHAPTER 26: THE GREY AREA

If there has been a constant in my life, it's the inevitability of shit hitting multiple fans after I've made some big resolution to buckle down and do the right thing. After my time in DC with Don, it couldn't have been clearer that I needed to be in a city with skyscrapers, smog, and more than one gay bar. But if the divorce had left Laura unhinged, the idea of me blowing black guys tore her out of the frame and sent her howling into the wind. A mere sighting of Dr. Adams, my former English professor, walking across campus would send her into paroxysms of scorn:

"I saw a *gay* on campus today!" she would snarl, subtext flashing behind her eyes.

"You're just mad he's not interested in you," I said one time, beyond tired of this shit. Another time, when I'd been out a bit longer, I got bolder: "You're just jealous I'm his type and you're not. Grow up."

Janelle's and my habit of telling her to grow up pissed her off. It happened about once a week, enough to keep her simmering and sometimes boiling over. As promised, Janelle had moved out on her eighteenth birthday... and ended up back home within a matter of months, gravely ill, covered head to toe with a red, itchy rash. There were endless trips to the doctor. No one could figure out what she had. She got tested for HIV but didn't have it. Mono, but the tests came back borderline (so did mine). Rocky Mountain spotted fever, but no, or so we thought at the time. Bedridden and unable to take care of herself, Janelle had to withdraw from classes (she had followed my example, withdrawn from Rose High, gotten a GED, and enrolled at Pitt Community College). Years later, she learned she had three separate strains of Lyme disease; she also learned she'd had Rocky Mountain spotted fever as well. Laura withheld the results... and, apparently, treatment. For some reason, Janelle didn't die. Somewhere along the way, Laura had decided she needed to be an assertive parent. Perhaps our demands that she grow up had finally inspired her to try. Perhaps her counselor had given her the idea. Perhaps one of her friends had. Perhaps she was beginning to get a measure of self-respect back after the divorce. No matter, but her abrupt transition to Aspirational Madame Dictator after years of crying and clinging and needing to be driven home after getting drunk and falling down in restaurants was never going to work. Once you abdicate parenthood, you can't have it back.

That fall, there was a lot of screaming.

"Whatever," I'd say, rolling my eyes.

"THAT'S RIGHT, WHATEVER! WHATEVER I SAY, YOU WILL DO!"

Then, from out of clear blue nowhere, she got the idea to take out life insurance policies on us.

"It's in case something happens," she said. "Because you never know."

I held my tongue until the day we went to the insurance agency to sign the papers.

"So you're doing this because I'm gay and Janelle's a slut,

and when we both die of AIDS, you'll cash in?" I asked.

Janelle cracked up. Laura and the insurance agent blanched.

That fall, I went for a lot of long drives, one time going all the way down to Bayview and taking the ferry across to Aurora, where Brian and Vanessa's river cottage had been. If I'd been thinking, I could have bought bread to feed the seagulls, as we'd done when I was a kid. According to Laura's story, Dick had enjoyed soaking the bread in beer before these trips. The family would toss lager-sodden slices of bread to the gulls and cackle as they got drunk and fell into the water, too hammered to fly. But my brain felt like a plate of scrambled eggs. During that period of time, I couldn't get enough of The Cure, Grace Jones, and Roxy Music. I'd listen to "In Between Days" and "I've Seen That Face Before (Libertango)" and "Same Old Scene" at full volume and pretend I was trying to escape from one of the JG Ballard novels I was glad I'd discovered but was also sort of appalled by. Later, to my surprise, I ended up talking to the Marine about her behavior. Ever since he'd started seeing Pam, who is now his second wife, he'd calmed down, so much so as to be almost unrecognizable.

"She's... always been like that," he said with some reluctance. "Deep down, she doesn't know who she is. She never has."

Janelle had been saying something similar for years. As one of her own counselors had pointed out, a person who goes by as many names as Laura did is bound to be confused. Her full name is Laura Mae "Anne Marie" Fulford Moore. The "Anne Marie" is in quotation marks on her birth certificate and was intended as a legal nickname. Granny called her that. Her high school friends called her Mae. Professionally, she went by Laura, and she signed checks as Laura M. Moore. The Marine called her Laura. It was as confusing as it sounds.

The Marine went on: "And she's angry with the world because she's never had a chance to find out. She was kept from doing the things she wanted to do in life, and now she takes it out on everyone else. All you can do is be patient with her and try to understand."

Said the guy who divorced her. But he had a point: he was talking about what *I* could do, not his own options. Problem was, the uproar had taken a toll. I'd already looked into legal emancipation, but it wouldn't serve any purpose that I could determine. I sat in German class or physics trying to plan my evening in order to minimize contact. Who could I hang out with so that I wouldn't have to go home until she'd gone to bed, and could they get beer? My own counselor framed the situation more starkly: I had toxic parents, to use the phrase that was popular then, and being mired in the middle of all *their* shit left me unable to deal with my own. The counselor shocked me with another observation, that Laura's groping and clinging and touching had crossed the line more than once and could be regarded as sexual abuse. There are things parents aren't meant to grab. At the very least, I ought to move into a dorm. Go home for a couple of meals. Do laundry during the day, while she was at work. Graduate, move as far away as possible, and don't come back except for visits.

Janelle recovered enough to move out and start working again, so I now bore the full force of the category 5 craziness. Granny even had to step in a couple of times and tell Laura to act like a grown woman. My goal was to graduate and get out, not to flunk out, whatever it took and whoever I had to hurt along the way. Then there was the money issue. Like too many other people, I got stuck in the credit-card trap of the late '80s and early '90s, when the big banks would send pre-approved cards to people they deemed likely to get in trouble. There was a lot of money to be made from late fees and high interest rates. I was working two part-time jobs and earning crap wages. There was no way I could afford to pay off the balance on my card; all I could do was make minimum payments, dog-paddling until my credit limit maxed out. When that happened, Chase Manhattan sold the debt into collections. The phone calls became a daily nuisance. I was already taking out student loans for my tuition. The idea of more debt terrified me. I thought it over and made a decision: I'd take a year off, work, pay down what I could, and then go back to ECU for my last year and a half of classes.

I worked at Kmart for a couple of months and quit, too bored and depressed to continue. As an adult, I feel uncomfortable writing this. I don't want to dishonor the work people in retail do. It's hard and often thankless. They're not paid enough. But I didn't have anything in common with my coworkers, there was nothing to talk about, and I faced a shitstorm of crazy as soon as I walked out the big glass doors. This wasn't supposed to be my future or my present. Kroger's was even worse: the manager couldn't stand me because I kept miscategorizing purchases when customers checked out. As she berated me, my mind wandered. How many of my classmates from S&M were at Harvard now, or Princeton? Or the cool little liberal arts colleges where, in truth, I should have ended up? Oberlin or Guilford College? Reed or U. of Richmond? Were they getting yelled at by a supermarket manager for not knowing the difference between Windex and Tide? Developing knee problems from standing all day came as a paintastic relief. Already on very thin ice for accepting a check drawn on a French bank account, I knew I wouldn't last much longer anyway, and if I had to sit through one more lecture on how I didn't understand that paper towels and plastic utensils required different codes on the cash register, I was going to cuss the bitch out in Latin and quit.

By now, my ASL was fluent enough that I could interpret classes, so I lucked into a gig at Pitt Community College. Back then, there was less awareness of repetitive strain injuries. Interpreters would work for hours without taking adequate breaks. Caught up in our shared delusions of how noble the profession was (far too many of us didn't notice how much this attitude annoyed deaf people), we'd gobble Advil for our aches and pains and keep going. Working all day brought in more money than I had made at the checkout counters, but by summer, I already had the first signs of damage in my hands, wrists, and shoulders. The first time you're in chronic pain, you don't believe it: you look at your extremities as if they don't belong to you, as if the pain isn't real, and you go on doing what you were doing before, making it worse. Within a matter of months, I went from relative normality to barely being able to sign my name on a check.

Even if Laura had sort of calmed down about the gay thing, lunacy reigned supreme. She'd lost so much weight you almost couldn't see her if she turned sideways, and, newly svelte, she capitalized on it. She chucked half her wardrobe and bought new stuff. She joined the Greenville Singles Club and went out line dancing. She declared a minor in Women's Studies and bought a lot of books with titles like *Lesbian Nuns*. Anxious around water all her life, she finally gathered her courage and took an introductory swimming course as an elective. She'd been slowly, steadily chipping away at her bachelor's degree for as long as I could remember, and had only a few courses left: math, which terrified her, and PE, whose swimming requirement terrified her even more. (Yes, there was a PE requirement, and unless you had a disability, you probably wouldn't graduate if you didn't know how to swim. I think that was sensible.) Once she got over her fear of water, she decided she loved it, perhaps for the same reason I once had. After dealing with her asshole boss all day, she could be alone with her thoughts.

Now that she'd moved on from her own *South Park*-style "YOU WILL RESPECT MAH AUTHORITAY!" phase, she decided she was going to be Workout Mama. She'd go to the pool, swim laps for an hour, come home, and pirouette around the house shadow-boxing and humming the theme from *Rocky*. She tried to convince me to go swimming with her, but I'd already been leered at in a Speedo enough in my early teens, thank you very much. Admittedly, this was a vast improvement over the previous, tipsy mess she'd been for the past, oh, I don't know, all my life, but I just wanted to flop on the sofa drinking beer and watching David Lynch and Peter Greenaway movies on the VCR with whoever felt like hanging out that night.

Having finally accepted that nothing with Adam was ever going to happen (well, we might have ended up in the sack a few times), I had moved on and started dating other guys. There was the guy who sold appliances at a local department store. That one lasted a few months. There was the cute Latino guy in the Navy; he was stationed down in Jacksonville, so we had to commute. There were a couple of fellow ECU students. If I met a guy at the Paddock Club and he didn't have a place to spend the night, I'd take him back to the Marine's house if he was at the beach for the weekend and shag my new friend in my father's bed. Now and then I even washed the sheets afterward. Being desperately lonely and a bit deranged, I'd go home with pretty much anyone who wanted me. And it seemed

251

people did. Some guys liked the dork look, I suppose. In fact, enough did that I began to think I should have a place of my own. Sooner or later, Laura would direct her craziness toward me again and I didn't want to be around for it. I didn't have clear plans for finishing college—I went back and forth on how much I believed the future was something I'd live to see—so it made sense to do what I could in the present, *with* the present.

That summer, I decided I'd maxed out on Laura's wailing and clinging but kind of neglected to mention I was moving out until the day I brought home a bunch of boxes and started packing all my shit. Torrence was now living with a guy named Jason, and they had a spare bedroom. Did I want to move in? It was an impulsive decision, but I was making enough to cover the rent and was going to have a nervous breakdown if I didn't create some more space. Perhaps in one of my mental sub-basements and maintenance tunnels, I understood that it wouldn't be a permanent arrangement. Nor was it even the best idea. Even if switching to interpreting (plus whatever other part-time gig I had on the side) meant I'd gotten a little income boost, it still didn't amount to much: fifteen or twenty dollars a week, maybe. Beer money. It used to be that when I went to bed at night, I struggled with awful truths and inner conflicts. I still did, but different ones now. Sexuality was no longer the issue, reality was. I was relieved that my life was finally about something other than the Olympics and/or the Ivy League and/or curing cancer and/or whatever the hell else people thought I was destined to do. I'd changed the narrative by burning it down, albeit accidentally. The problem with intelligence is other people's expectations. It's not an insurance policy against screwing up, nor is it a permanent exemption from normality. But when the expectations you've grown up with become your own, urging you toward more and better and brighter, cash registers and delivery trucks will never be enough. I understood this when I moved out, and by the time I had to move back into Laura's house, the truth about what I had to do burned like white phosphorus. But first, though:

This guy stopped by to see Jason one afternoon. An ex of his, I think, or a former fuck-buddy. Black, mid-20s, a few years older than me. Average-looking, kind of lean. I remember his cock but not his face or his name. Let's call him Milton. Jason was on his way to work, so Milton didn't stay long. He lingered on his way out, though.

"I've got a bag, if you want to hang out," he said, punctuating this with a long, penetrating look. "I can come by later."

Being an idiot and rather horribly literal at times, I didn't get it.

"Umm, sure?" For once, I wasn't working that night, and if he wanted to come back and smoke a bowl, I wasn't going to say no. I didn't take his offer seriously, and had almost forgotten when I heard the doorbell a few hours later.

It was either really premium weed or he'd spiked it. I have no idea what we talked about, although we must have done something between hits on the pipe other than look at each other with sex (him) and damaged cluelessness (me) in mind. I'm pretty sure we had a beer or two, and I'm equally sure you have guessed where this is going. He wanted to fool around. Too high to object, I was fine with it until his unilateral decision to fuck me. I hadn't been on the receiving end before and was in no hurry to try, certainly not with some random guy I'd just met. But how was I supposed to explain that I wasn't into it without sounding like I wasn't into him for crappy awful white-people reasons? Caught up in a psychedelic mesh of

THC and Southern Racism Processing, I literally didn't know what was going on until the inevitable was already happening. He paused in the proceedings long enough to put on a condom, and, thoroughly baked, I was still deep in my own head when he pushed me back, grabbed my legs, pushed them up toward my shoulders, and tried to shove his cock into me. If you've ever tried to force an eggplant through the eye of a needle, you might have an idea how well this worked out. I'm actually not exaggerating as much as you might think, either. It hurt and I yelled. He kept trying, and the pain was like an uncharted prime number. Buzz gone, my language skills came back and I switched to profanities. I started to struggle, trying to get out from under him. He'd jabbed at me with his dick enough times—and I think it went in far enough the first time to clear the way for more intimate damage—that my ass felt sore and bruised. I was so distracted by the fact that it was happening to me that I couldn't actually believe that it was happening to me. This is what happens when you spend most waking hours quite far outside of your own head.

Scowling, he asked, "I thought you were gonna make this worth my while?"

"I'm going to the bathroom to clean up," I said.

While I was in there, I took a quick shower, more to get the smell of him off me than to clean up any bodily fluids. Neither of us had come. I was just grossed out. My head spun with questions and weed. *Was that a rape? Did that guy just rape me? Did it start being rape when I stopped being into it, or is this some kind of grey area?* The answers are clearer now, but almost three decades ago, not so much. After the shower, I returned my bedroom with a towel around my waist. Milton was gone. So, I discovered, was the cash I kept in a small box on a bookshelf.

254

Not that much, about $75, but again, when you're earning three and a half bucks an hour and the guy who stole it from you just held you down and kind of raped you, it was an insult on top of a literal injury.

In hot mindless spasm of rage, I punched the wall. My fist went straight through the drywall, leaving a dusty hole several inches across.

"You're paying for that," Jason said when he got home a couple of hours later.

I looked for an extra second at his hair transplants. Little blond sprigs on his scalp. He was scowling.

"Of course," I said. "As soon as I get the money back that your *friend* stole from me."

Jason talked to Milton, who denied everything.

I didn't tell the Marine why I needed his advice on how to patch a wall you've punched a hole in, and when he came over, he looked at me with a twinge of respect I had never previously seen. *Was this what it took all along?* I wondered. Past the point of caring, I let go of it. He filled in the hole by himself and left me a small can of paint and a paintbrush for when the plaster dried. To his credit, he didn't ask questions.

I didn't tell Laura why I needed to move back in, either. I covered it up with my decision to re-enroll at ECU and get it over with once and for all, whatever it took.

I didn't go to the police, either. It didn't even cross my mind. I was gay, he was black, we were stoned, and it was the South. Even when I told Torrence and Jason what happened, I left the saltiest parts out.

If that year was all I could expect from life without finishing college, it was time for me to be done.

CHAPTER 27: A YEAR OF ENDINGS

My final year at ECU, and in Greenville, really started the summer before. The couple of months I spent living with Torrence and Jason ended in late spring, and by the time my birthday rolled around, I was back in Laura's house and strangely relieved. I didn't tell her what had happened, although she seemed to suspect something had. As much as I could, I pushed it out of my head. I blamed myself anyway, so there didn't seem to be much to say. I re-enrolled at ECU (it only took a phone call to the registrar), submitted my student-loan applications, and that was basically that.

I don't think any of my friends—mostly the ones I'd met through ECU's LGBT student organization, which I had somehow ended up running—realized at the time we were having one of those summers that we would name in retrospect. But we did: the Naked Summer. We kept breaking into different apartment complexes' swimming pools to go skinny-dipping, usually after a night at the Paddock. One night, most of the crowd decided to streak through their neighborhood, the area just south of what is now called the Warehouse District. I didn't join them, but I did go pick them up in the Marine's Oldsmobile afterward (he and Pam went to the beach most weekends and would sometimes leave me one of the cars) and drive them back to the house, never mentioning that I'd stuffed his car full of nude college students.

Toward the end of the Naked Summer, one of our Fearless Adventure Team decided she'd had enough of college and dropped out to become a stripper. A local roadhouse held an amateur night, so we dutifully trooped up to the grotty north side of town to watch Roxie dance. (By this point we'd all seen her boobs before, and once during a game of Truth or Dare, seen her turn a cartwheel in the nude. This is how we learned that she was having her period. The tampon string fluttered in the breeze between her legs.) Her performance went smashingly until the manager rushed out in a panic, interrupting the routine to instruct her not to touch herself Down There while she was dancing. Another time, after a night at the Fallout Shelter in Raleigh, we ended up in the pool at some apartment building in a part of town I didn't know at all. My friend Sean and I were feeling a bit conspicuous that night and kept our clothes on. (Or rather, I kept my clothes on because Sean did.) Perhaps it was just as well. Cops arrived, and Roxie rescued us by bounding up to them still naked and dripping, playing innocent:

"Why, officers!" (Jiggle, jiggle.) "We didn't know we were doing anything wrong!" (Jiggle, jiggle.) "Please don't arrest us." (Jiggle, jiggle.)

One of the cops was obviously a dyke and couldn't take her eyes off Roxie's tits. We were let go with a warning and laughed the whole way back to Greenville.

Not long after the fall semester started, our cat Cupcake had to be put down. We'd had her since she was a kitten. In typical Southern fashion, she mostly lived outdoors and in the basement/garage at Brook Valley. We weren't supposed to let

Cupcake and Muffin (another cat we adopted when she turned up on our doorstep as a kitten) indoors but did it anyway. Both cats were black with white markings: Cupcake was a standard American shorthair, and Muffin might have had a little Persian in the mix. She was fluffier. She disappeared after a few years, though, possibly catnapped after a yard sale. Cupcake's mood improved once Muffin vanished. Cats are like that. But as time went by and our family drama worsened, we all disappeared into our own damaged heads. Laura still fed her, but we didn't spend as much time with her as we once had. Cupcake would sometimes come meet me on the steps at Laura's house when I got home at night, and she'd sit in my lap and purr. Eventually she'd wander off, and I'd go inside.

I've always believed our misery took a toll on her. It wasn't neglect in the worst sense: we kept her fed, we played with her when we remembered to, and she was off doing cat things much of the time. She wasn't the type of cat who'd come when you called. But I had a nagging feeling we weren't doing enough, and then one day when I got home from class, I heard her meowing in the back yard. She lay on the back lawn in a shady spot, and there was an open, bloody hole in her flank almost the size of a nickel. Some other animal had bitten her and taken out a big chunk.

I rushed indoors to call Laura at work. When I explained the situation, she brushed it off: "Oh, cats get cuts and bites all the time. I'll look at it when I get home."

"No. You don't understand. There's a *hole* in her side. She needs to go to the vet *now*."

The only reason I didn't take her myself—and I have wrestled with this—is that she seemed to like Laura more than the rest of us. (Laura has always been excellent with animals.

Plants, too.) I was afraid that if I tried to pick Cupcake up and take her to the vet, she wouldn't cooperate and might bite me. She was in a lot of pain and I didn't want to make her injuries worse.

Laura got home, took one look at her, and told me to get a towel. I drove to the vet's office and she held Cupcake swaddled in that towel, and talked to her in a soft voice. Fortunately, the vets were able to see her right away; they took her in, stitched up the wound, and gave her antibiotics.

Cupcake never really recovered. I think the injury was too severe, and as soon as she had some energy back, she chewed the stitches out. The wound had partially healed, so at least there wasn't a gaping hole in her side as there had been before. But as the days passed, her coat lost its luster and her eyes grew dull. We all knew where this was headed.

On a Saturday morning a few days later, Laura decided that the time had come. Janelle met her at the vet's office. I didn't want to go. I couldn't do it. I couldn't absorb any more tears and didn't want to shed my own in front of anyone else. After trying to convince me for a few minutes, Laura left in exasperation. About an hour later, she was back, ashen.

This is the worst thing I have ever done. I will never forgive myself for it. The humans in my life have largely deserved what I've done to them, but that cat deserved better.

Buckling down and doing the work doesn't make for compelling reading, but after Cupcake met her sad, shitty end, I'd had enough of pretty much everyone and everything. I stayed home most Friday and Saturday nights instead of going out. I read; I rented movies; I did homework. I wrote.

About midway through the fall semester, Terry, a deaf man I'd been dating over in Wilson, about forty-five minutes away from Greenville, was diagnosed with full-blown AIDS. He'd gone back home to Tennessee for the holidays. His parents took one look at him and took him straight from the airport to the hospital. We'd always been very safe, so I was not at risk, but this happened a couple of months after Warren died of Hodgkin's lymphoma. It came up out of nowhere and he was gone in a matter of months. Terry spent about a week in an inpatient ward before he was allowed to go home. His family insisted he move back to Tennessee—to die, basically. He came back to Wilson just long enough to pack up his apartment and have final dinners with friends. I slept on the floor that night. No one else in the house heard me cry myself to sleep.

Through all of this, I stayed fairly quiet and focused. I stayed in most weekends. I hauled my grades back out of the doldrums. Had this skill been there all along? I thought not.

During Fall Break, I took the train up to DC to visit Jim, who'd graduated a year earlier and gotten a job with the Census Bureau. He'd lucked into a great house-sitting gig for an aunt and uncle who were out of the country. With the money he wasn't spending on rent (even on a comfortable General Service salary, he couldn't have afforded that mansion in Bethesda), he bought a blue Mazda Miata, which made him the coolest person I knew. I don't know what scared me more that long weekend, him dragging me to a number of restaurants to try foreign cuisines for the first time (Thai, Korean, Ethiopian, and Vietnamese), or his mad idea to go skydiving. We went. He did it. I didn't, although he tried to talk me into it. I'd already had enough death, but I couldn't tell him that in so many words.

Lacking any sort of plan for what I'd do after graduation, I applied for Gallaudet University's master's program in speech pathology. It wasn't that I wanted to be a speech pathologist.

I just couldn't think of anything else to do with myself, and it would get me to DC. I looked into joining the Peace Corps, but ultimately didn't. No one with my digestive issues needs to be living rough in the developing world.

One night at dinner toward the end of that final spring semester, Janelle and I were having dinner with the Marine and Pam. After transferring to ECU, Janelle had taken one or two ASL classes. She caught my eye and glanced down, meaning for me to look down at her lap. Below the table, she fingerspelled: ROGER AND I ARE GETTING MARRIED ON SATURDAY. The whites of her eyes were not bloodshot, and her pupils were their normal size.

I had to pretend nothing was happening. So many dinners had been like this, a dance of normalcy done by clumsy people who knew they were anything but normal. I had applied for a couple of jobs, so we talked about that. No real expectations, but it was at least an opportunity. With a recession on, very few people seemed to be finding jobs in their majors. One friend's father had lost his job and taken work as a short-order cook in a barbecue restaurant just to keep money coming in; others found themselves in unwanted early retirements. After dinner, Janelle told me the rest of the details: she and Roger, her Marine boyfriend-now-fiancé, had decided to make it legal. They were living together in an apartment in New Bern. Janelle was commuting back to Greenville for classes and work, and he was commuting down to the air station at Cherry Point. They'd just gotten approved for a mortgage and would be buying a little house, and… she'd have military health care! Unconvinced she was madly in love, I just looked at her for a moment or two. Getting married at nineteen didn't seem like the smartest idea. But then, who was I to argue with insurance and equity?

They had a sweet, simple ceremony officiated by the Carteret County Justice of the Peace over in Morehead City. There were about ten people there. The ceremony was over in less than twenty minutes. Afterward, we went to Sanitary Seafood. Champagne, I discovered, is great when you're eating fried shrimp.

I'm not sure how Laura found out about the wedding. I thought I'd been discreet, leaving the house, but she confronted me with it a week later.

"So you're still spying," I said.

This time, she didn't start caterwauling about her right maintain to a constant poking, prying, prodding presence in our lives. Even if she had, I was no longer reacting with the anger I once had. It just encouraged her, as the Marine pointed out. Better to keep all interactions as brief and emotion-free as possible.

If there was any celebration at the end of the semester, it was the day Hank and I drove down to the beach. The war in Iraq had wound down, and one of his friends had brought back special cigarettes: tobacco soaked in opium and wrapped in hemp. We didn't have anything in particular in mind, just an afternoon down at the beach. We visited with the Marine and Pam for a bit, then walked across the street to the Atlantic side of the island (they'd built the place on the sound side to give it shelter from hurricanes). That day more than anything sticks out in my head as the day college ended. We still had another week or two of classes, and graduation would take place in early July. I actually had to complete one final course over the summer, but students in that situation were allowed to graduate anyway. There was a lot of "We did it" and "Took us long enough" and "Want another hit?" As far as Hank knew, he'd be going back

262

to Statesville, his hometown, and I'd be interviewing for one of those jobs, with the state rehabilitation-services agency's office up in Winston-Salem. I didn't get into Gallaudet's MA program but wasn't too concerned about it. If I got the job, great, I'd work for a while and see where things went. If not, then... I'd do something else.

A few weeks later, I graduated. Because ECU is such a large university, the ceremony is held in the football stadium. Far too many people melted in their black nylon graduation gowns because they had put on suits and formal dresses. Let them have their decorum: I wore jeans and a purple T-shirt, and to be a little vulgar and rebellious, I wore a studded leather cock ring around one (bony) wrist. I'm pretty sure no one else knew what it actually was. As for that last psychology course—either statistics or testing, I've forgotten—I trudged through it and passed.

A couple of weeks after *that*, I got a letter from Vocational Rehabilitation congratulating me on my successful interview and inviting me to start at the beginning of September. Having always worried I was basically unhireable, I couldn't quite believe the news, and the preparations resembled the ones seven years earlier, the previous time I'd left Greenville. I had to drive up to Winston and find an apartment. (I chose a two-bedroom piece of shit almost directly across the street from my office. For once, this was a mistake the Marine didn't try to keep me from making, even though I could tell he thought the place was a dump.) Having sold my last car, I needed another one. That was sorted out; I bought a white Toyota hatchback—with air conditioning this time. The Marine, Laura, and Sean helped me move.

This was the beginning of one of the loneliest, most bizarre, and most boring parts of my life, the two years I spent in Winston-Salem and Greensboro, but in a strange way, it was also one of the best parts. I had done it, burnt it all to the ground, and begun to construct some semblance of a life out of the ashes. Perhaps not a *normal* life, because that was never in the cards and never would be. But it was a life that would be on my own terms, which was more than enough. It was a start.

AFTERWORD

I have known since childhood that I would write this book, although the reasons behind it have evolved. I'll be honest: my original motivation was revenge. Then I grew up. Several times along the way, I changed my mind about trying to write this. I saw myself primarily as a fiction writer, and I worried that if I were to tell my origin story, I risked emptying the well, so to speak. But I'd just finished the PhD, a process that involved setting aside my longstanding policy/superstition about working in private: sharing that manuscript with my supervisor one chapter at a time didn't kill the story. I got it done. Passed my viva. Learned a few lessons. Reflected on this story, and realized it could stand on its own. I've had an unusual life, and to borrow a bit of wisdom from recovery programs, you're only as sick as your secrets. I spent much of my teens and twenties unable to talk about these experiences. I'd like to think that I've gained enough perspective to tell the story now with no agenda other than the telling. I hope I have succeeded.

As you'd expect, most of the names in this book have been changed. In my parents' case, this is a privacy issue. Although a number of the people who read the book will know who they are, the world has come unhinged. I don't want this book to inspire trolls and lunatics to track them down. Other people's names are, of course, used with permission. Some requested that I use pseudonyms. In other cases, the people had passed away and I didn't think it would be appropriate to use their real names. Sometimes I did; sometimes not.

The circumstances surrounding my paternal grandparents' deaths are a matter of public record. As with my parents, I changed their names out of respect for distant living relatives who might not want their own lives brought under the spotlight in this way. Interestingly, my sister found references in online news archives after reading this book in manuscript form. Among other things, she confirmed that our paternal grandfather had a mistress and had at least two children with her. Although I have no particular interest in meeting these half-uncles or aunts and any children they might have, this discovery says a lot about why I needed to tell this story in the first place. The surprises keep coming.

To wrap up this bit of text, I'd like to give thanks where they're due. My sister helped flesh out some of the details of the story and kindly consented for me to leave the unflattering bits in. Simon Yuen and our cat Moosh Monster (aka the Fur Bomb, aka Dangerfloof, aka Goddamn It Are You Underfoot Again, Are You Trying to Kill Me?) were there throughout and did much to keep body and mind together. Sven Davisson at Rebel Satori Press deserves awards and gratitude and frankincense and myrrh for publishing this. Jerry Wheeler, Vince Liaguno, Jim Holt, and Manos Apostolidis all read earlier drafts of the manuscript and offered feedback. I have a nagging suspicion someone else did too, but the sand is out of the hourglass now. Michael and Zak Zakar kindly offered promotional blurbs (if you don't follow them on Instagram, you probably should). Mattilda Bernstein Sycamore was one of the first to encourage me to write it in the first place (and will probably not recall doing so). My terrific new colleagues at Falmouth University have done a great deal to make arriving solo in the UK during the pandemic and immediately after the ordeal in Hong Kong a lot less nightmarish than it could have been. And Calvin Malham warrants a great deal more than a one-sentence shout-out. Finally, there are any number of people I didn't mention in the book, either by name or pseudonym, not because their contributions didn't matter but because there wasn't room: friends who were there, teachers who were supportive, strangers who intervened. In the course of writing this thing, I've come to realize that Greenville was much smaller back in the day, and more people knew what was going on in my family than I realized. There's been a lot of help along the way, sometimes in the open and sometimes behind the scenes. Thank you.

Truro, Cornwall
February 2022